PRIMORDIAL CHAOS

To Danny
all the best!
In Chaos
Dave

PRIMORDIAL CHAOS

WRITINGS AND RITUALS THEN & NOW

DAVE LEE

THE UNIVERSE MACHINE
NORWICH

First published 2023 by The Universe Machine, Norwich

ISBN 978-1-7398688-6-4

Contents

Acknowledgements

Dedicated to the people who helped me grow in magick: Learners who were my teachers, teachers who taught but didn't know how to learn anything new; those who did both.

Introduction

This selection of writings reflects my life in magic over the last four-and-a-half decades. It is arranged in four parts.

Part 1, 'Primal Chaos', starts in the chaos magic scene. I was part of this from the beginning, as a founder member of the first IOT group in England which was based in West Yorkshire and ran from 1980 to '82.

Today, over 40 years later, I'm still working in the IOT. Chaos magic is alive, evolving and changing; despite the warnings I've seen every few years since about 1987 that it's dead. Some of the core chaos magic ideas have influenced new communities, sparking shared practices and philosophies that are needed more than ever in this traumatized, 'post-truth' world where people are getting into magical thinking without any critical perspectives.

This early part also reprises a piece I wrote when I worked with Phoenix Light Lodge in 1981–82, the strand other than chaos magic of my early magical education. This is actually the earliest published article in this collection.

Most of my magical life has focused on practice. Spells for myself, of course, but much of my practice has been—and still is—to do with facilitating group magic. The attraction of group magic for me was and is manifold, but it's probably the prospect of sharing interesting weirdness that drew me in in the first place. At age 17 I heard some Jefferson Airplane lyrics about activities that have not yet been given names,[1] and decided that what I wanted in life was lots of exciting, weird experiences. Later, I found that 'doing magic' fitted that ambition quite well. That enthusiastically neophiliac approach to life works much better when you have other people around you, acting as mirrors for each other in evaluating weird experiences and non-standard ontologies. Sharing the weirdness with others boosts it but also acts to ground and balance it. With powerful magic, big shifts in your cosmology can occur, and these can be disturbing: *Am I going madder than I want to be, or am I seeing things more clearly?* This is where the feedback from other people engaging in intense weirdness is really important.

Then there's the unique quality of egregore entity work (more of which in Part 4), plus the extraordinary power that can be raised in group workings. Not to mention the sheer fun that can be had when we work with other people who are willing to step out of consensus reality.

---

[1] 'Wild Tyme' on the album *After Bathing at Baxter's*.

Although I began to keep a magical diary in 1978, which I mark as the beginning of my daily commitment to a magical life, I regarded my approach as experimental, so I didn't actually start writing about magic for publication for a few more years. I waited till I was ready to present what felt like a fresh viewpoint based on personal experience.

Before I started that diary, I had several intense magical experiences, mostly in my late teens and involving LSD. Psychedelics were the beginning of my re-entry into the magical thinking I'd abandoned at about four years old. I explore that connection in **Part 2**.

I always tried to find the best teachers for anything I was keen on learning. Pete Carroll was my early mentor in chaos magic, and another two magicians from my days in Phoenix Light gave important inputs to the more mystical side of my magical life. In the mid-1990s I extended my fascination with the mysteries of place and the origins of cultures by beginning to study and practice the 'Northern Mysteries'. I joined the Rune-Gild because they are the only organization I have yet found which brings to that work a respect for both the history and the magic. Some of that story I tell in **Part 3**. (Part 3 is the shortest section, because much of the Northern Mysteries material I've created is either published elsewhere or overlaps with other categories, so it's in a different part of the book.)

In **Part 4** I gather together a few of the many public magical presentations I've done over the years and write about the scenes around those workings. I also present some entities that are still being worked with, which you can engage with if you wish.

What justifies this sort of collection? Occultural history and nostalgia, for a start. These pieces are now mostly out of print, and some people who missed them first time round might actually want to read them!

Then there's my own narrative. None of us is just one thing, one current, one scene. Or rather it's very sad if that is what we think we are; a clear example of Sartre's 'bad faith'. The book is divided up into themes rather than strict chronological eras, because a range of my esoteric interests are represented here, and they don't normally get lumped together like this. After most of a lifetime of those interests—psychedelic experience, ritual magic, energy work, Northern magic, and the various communities involved—I am still puzzling out how it all fits together, still struggling to articulate even to myself what is important to me about those scenes and practices. One overarching theme of my magical life has been about facilitating groups of people to do weird things, and this is reflected in the structure of this book. You'll notice that Part 1 is the longest of the four parts; most of my magical writings were written as a 'chaos magician'. Taken together with Part 4, the public parts of my magical work, this makes up half the book.

Therefore much of the book is a memoir, of my times and the times of the scenes that inspired me, using these old texts as markers in the timeline. It's also a product of an increasingly urgent need to articulate magic for this scary and precarious era. Magic may be the only thing we have left, outwardly as the 'poor man's sword' of resistance, and inwardly as the path where our own transformation is exactly what we need to achieve, and, maybe all that we can achieve?

It was all the more enjoyable to republish these pieces together with some reflections on how my thinking has changed. I hope you enjoy them too.

Part 1: Magical Writings from 1979 Onwards

The Lamp of Thoth

Chaos Magic crystallized as a current with the publication of two books in 1978, both issued by Ray Sherwin's Morton Press. Sherwin's own *The Book of Results* was a small booklet with a set of instructions for doing your own sigils, with minimal metaphysics. It no doubt encouraged some people to have a go at making up their own magical spells. Pete Carroll's *Liber Null* was a complete overview of practical magic. Those two books, *Liber Null* and *The Book of Results*, seeded the interest that led to the formation of the first Chaos Magic groups, notably in West Yorkshire.

That's one origin tale, and it's not the only one. Pete Carroll wrote of a slightly earlier proto-Chaos magical community in North London, the Stoke Newington Sorcerers, which included Gerald Suster and Charles Brewster, both now gone from this world.[2] Other writers have published fragments of interviews indicating another source of the current, a goat-roast in Deptford.[3] A fourth story returns the origin to Yorkshire, with the so-called Whitby Conclave. According to this latter account,[4] the whole plot was hatched by a group of people including Lionel Snell in 1979, on a social scene which included the founders of the original Starchild occult supply shop. This last story sets the origin a little too late though.

Whichever of these origins is 'true', the idea of a current emerging from a social scene is crucial here. Musician Brian Eno came up with a helpful concept for looking at artistic history, which can also be applied to the esoteric world: the *scenius*. A scenius is a social scene with an advanced discourse going on which enables the emergence of a new perspective. This new perspective then manifests via the work of some individuals on that scene, the most articulate or the pushiest, who then get the credit, even though the ideas were current in that discourse community.

Looked at this way, the scenius that chaos magic emerged from was a cluster of thinkers and practitioners, of whom the first to publish the core ideas would have been Lionel Snell, aka Ramsey Dukes, aka Lea and Angerford. Snell's 1974 publication *SSOTBME* (*Sex Secrets Of The Black*

---

[2] Charlie Brewster's only published writings, as far as I'm aware, are in *Liber Cyber*, an extraordinary collection of anecdotes from 1991. Publisher, Ecliptica.

[3] Hawkins J. (1996). *Understanding Chaos Magic*, Capall Bann Publishing.

[4] http://the-philosophers-stone.com/articles/whitby/whitby.htm

Magicians Exposed) was the first book to lay down a model of magic that didn't pretend that modern scientific culture had never happened; it was an unapologetic embrace of magic but couched in terms that the modern reader could appreciate. This book opened up the possibility of multi-model thinking, including magical thinking.

That kind of thinking is of course closely allied to a current that was developing on the other side of the Atlantic—the 'multi-model agnosticism' of Robert Anton Wilson. This approach acknowledges that any perspective we have on the world is bound to be part of a massive, inclusive gestalt, a whole bunch of beliefs about the world that come as a complete nested set, every belief implying every other. These sets of world-describing (or world-creating) beliefs are known as *reality tunnels*. Once we recognize that we are in a particular reality tunnel which limits everything we can think—for instance Atheist Scientism, Buddhism, Marxism, or Catholicism—we are then free to shift to another. This is an essential skill for anyone who wants to live their life fully, honouring all their experiences, rather than deciding that a particular experience can't be real because it doesn't sit easily with mainstream culture's dominant religion, Scientism.

It's worth noting here that Scientism is distinct from science. Science is a tremendously useful methodology that applies logic to physical phenomena and enables new technologies. Its approach to truth is, at its best, open-ended and non-dogmatic. Scientism, on the other hand, is a religion. Its adherents declare that science is the only way of approaching truth and that any experiences that cannot be explained (or explained away) by scientific truth as it stands today must be invalid, or even delusions or hallucinations. Scientism believers (such as its high priest Richard Dawkins) make statements which are clearly metaphysical but which we are supposed to accept as scientific. I go into Scientism below, particularly in the essay 'Three Thurses For Thee' in Part 3. To return to multi-model agnosticism, this is also important for any magician who values their mental health in this post-truth age, as a solvent of crazy beliefs. Applied to magic, multi-model thinking went way beyond what the post-Crowley current called Thelema was doing with belief. It was radical, in the genuine sense of looking right into the roots of magical technique.

The success of chaos magic in West Yorkshire had two main drivers: the existence of the Sorcerer's Apprentice in Leeds, an occult supply shop which also published a couple of the early Chaos Magic books and distributed *Liber Null* and *The Book of Results*, and the hospitality of Ray Sherwin in East Morton, a village just outside Bradford. The SA was (it's now mail order only) a dark emporium, fragrant with heavy incenses, on a back street in a disreputable part of town. Run by Chris Bray, it was a peculiar hybrid. On the one hand, it was the best magical bookshop you've ever seen, with delicious incenses and some impressive artefacts. (The Boscastle Museum of Witchcraft and Magic has a number of fine magical implements sold by the SA. I made one of their Goetic wands.)

The other side of the SA reminded one of a slightly tacky fancy goods shop locked into a permanent Halloween theme. The SA were a great resource for the local occult scene and things really started moving when they started hosting coffee mornings on Saturdays.

These events formed the setting for my personal introduction to the IOT. You walked into the tiny one-storey retail unit that looked like it had survived a number of urban renewals. You paid your money (into an honesty box) and poured water from the kettle into a paper cup with instant coffee and dried milk in it. The décor was unrelieved black. This had been the SA's main shop unit before it moved into the slightly more impressive premises next door. I lived about ten minutes walk away, in a house full of crazy young magical experimentalists like myself, so I was a regular attendee.

Never underestimate the power of the right kind of soiree to nurture new ideas. The SA coffee mornings were an astonishingly fruitful nexus of contacts. People who grew up in the online world may not realise how important such meeting places were. It was there I met Ray Sherwin and later Pete Carroll. Other luminaries include the remarkable Richard Bartle-Birtelli, a gentleman who illustrated that magicians didn't have to be in their 20s. This was a man who'd survived the Second World War and ended up living in Dewsbury in West Yorkshire teaching art. At that time, I'd never met a magician who had survived so long and was still doing magic. He came and gave a talk at the Leeds University Union Occult Society, another group I was involved in founding, as I shall tell in a later memoir.

In 1978 I started keeping a magical diary. One of my first entries described the consecration of the first robe I made. I took the first bus of the day to Ilkley, walked up onto the moor, along a ravine called Spicey Gill and washed the robe in a stream at dawn. I was rewarded with the sight of the slender cigar-body of a great dragonfly hovering over the stream as I finished, its wings iridescing in the morning light. By starting a diary and making a robe I'd kicked my magical life up a notch or two, and the appearance of that dragonfly, in my wide-open state, felt like a blessing on that new magical life. If asked when I started practicing magic, that month, October 1978, is often my answer.

The Carthorse, The Orchestra and The God of Silence

This piece is the only substantial text from my time with Phoenix Light and it's the oldest piece here. My life in the Phoenix Light era involved a lot of travel; my fellow group members lived in Southampton, my girlfriend lived in Sheffield and I lived in Leeds. Fortunately, hitch-hiking was easy in those days, and brought some interesting experiences. Sometimes, people went out of their way to give me a better lift, miles out of their way. Other times, they provided some rare entertainment, the kind you can only get by putting yourself in random situations. Waiting in the snow outside Southampton, I was picked up by a station wagon. I was carrying a rucksack, and the driver invited me to drop it in the back, on top of a long parcel wrapped in dark grey blankets. As we got underway, it turned out that the driver worked for an undertaker's firm. He had just driven back from France, and the bundle in the back was the corpse of an English client returning home. Wondering if I'd been disrespectful, I asked him if it was OK that my rucksack was on top of the body. 'No problem,' he said. 'It's not going to bother him.'

At that time I was intensely absorbed in studying Crowley's *Liber AL*, and wanted to come at what was obviously a prophetic document from a fresh angle rather than the usual interpretations of the card-carrying Thelemic community. Like a few other people who wanted to bring something to that discussion, I got focused on the mystery of the verses in Chapter 2 which in the facsimile have a line veering across the page, those verses that are so suddenly unfettered from the relative clarity of the rest of AL:

> *75. Aye! listen to the numbers & the words:*
> *76. 4 6 3 8 A B K 2 4 A L G M O R 3 Y X 24 89 R P S T O V A L. What meaneth this, o prophet? Thou knowest not; nor shalt thou know ever. There cometh one to follow thee: he shall expound it. But remember, o chosen one, to be me; to follow the love of Nu in the star-lit heaven; to look forth upon men, to tell them this glad word.*

What a temptation, to be the one who will follow Crowley! One of the groups called the AA, led by Jim Lees in the Midlands, devised a scheme they called the 'Qabalah of AL'. I heard about this because the AA people took over from Ray Sherwin the name of his magazine *The New Equinox*, then changed it to *The British Journal of Magick*. They published a number of items about the use of numerical keys in their rituals. Their gematria worked on attributing the numbers 1–26 to a re-ordering of the English alphabet, starting with A and then jumping 11 places to L and so on, until you've gone right round the alphabet. This fits in with the word AL, which is also part of the 'puzzle' string ALGMOR. I found this intriguing so I started my own numerological studies on *Liber AL*. I showed my results to my co-workers in Phoenix Light, and Marion—amateur mathematician and gematria fan—suggested trying other odd numbers that would generate further unique sequences.

Well, that soon escalated. We found there were 12 possible gematrias that used similar jump-sequences, and we started putting some magical words through all of them. We looked for new patterns—different patterns emerging within different gematrias, and any patterns of correspondence that held up across more than one gematria.

This kind of behaviour will not make much sense to anyone who has never got obsessed with gematria.

Then Mike, who worked as a software developer, decided we needed to take it up to the next level, by coding a programme that would sum any word over all the gematrias. This climaxed in a caffeine-fuelled 15-hour coding marathon at Mike's firm in Southampton, during which I mostly just made suggestions and coffee. That fine frenzy led to a dictionary of 666 words, each with twelve numerations, a substantial pile of green-striped fanfold computer printout.

What in the end did we get out of it? Whiffs of insight, synchronicities involving car number plates and so on, and a kind of frazzled manic state, where synchronicities and minor cerebral gnoses were commonplace. It was years before I could bring myself to touch gematria again.

The title for this piece came from a suggestion of Marion's. She was a crossword compiler and of course the connection between gematria and anagrams is obvious; she pointed out that 'carthorse' is an anagram of 'orchestra'.

THE CARTHORSE, THE ORCHESTRA AND THE GOD OF SILENCE: NUMBERING THE LETTERS OF THE ALPHABET

By Dave Lee, Mike Parker and Marion Parker
Originally published in Lamp of Thoth, 1981

'Every number is infinite, there is no difference' Liber AL, I:4

INTRODUCTION:

The correspondence of numbers with words and letters has been most extensively explored with Hebrew gematria. Magical Hebrew is a dead language, immune to change, fixed long ago by rabbinical tradition. In attempting English gematria we must surely bear in mind that English is the biggest and most complex language ever to have been spoken on this planet, and that it is still evolving. Can we really accept that such a fluid structure can be attributed to a rigid, single-valued system? The discovery of the 'Qabalah of AL' was a powerful lead-in to the exegesis of the book from which it was derived, Crowley's *Book of the Law*. However, it has been shown (Marion Parker's letter in *L.O.T.5* and her article in *L.O.T.7*) that a five-based system is also workable, and we hope that this article goes some way to demonstrating that twelve gematrias of this type can be used in a complementary, interlocked fashion. We have used examples from *AL* in this article, but have found these systems equally useful in corresponding other magical areas of language.

CHOOSING FROM THE ENORMOUS NUMBER OF GEMATRIAS:

Using the numbers 1–26 gives us 26 factorial, or about $4x10^{26}$ gematrias. This unwieldy quantity can be reduced by fixing the values of single letters to single numbers; fixing one letter reduces it by a factor of 26, fixing two, by (26x25) and so on. A more fruitful method of selection is to employ only simple series of intuitive meaningfulness. The *Qabalah of AL* does this by fixing A as 1 and going round the alphabet as a cycle in jumps of 11 letters. The gematria of 5 also does this, and in fact any odd number between 1 and 25 (with the exception of 13) can be used in this way. This was our starting point, generating 12 gematrias which are structurally interrelated, as shown in the following square:

BASE	B Z	C Y	D X	E W	F V	G U	H T	I S	J R	K Q	L P	M O
1	2	3	4	5	6	7	8	9	10	11	12	13
25	26	25	24	23	22	21	20	19	18	17	16	15
3	10	19	2	11	20	3	12	21	4	13	22	5
23	18	9	26	17	8	25	16	7	24	15	6	23
5	22	17	12	7	2	23	18	13	8	3	24	19
21	6	11	16	21	26	5	10	15	20	25	4	9
7	16	5	20	9	24	13	2	17	6	21	10	25
19	12	23	8	19	4	15	26	11	22	7	18	3
9	4	7	10	13	16	19	22	25	2	5	8	11
17	24	21	18	15	12	9	6	3	26	23	20	17
11	20	13	6	25	18	11	4	23	16	9	2	21
15	8	15	22	3	10	17	24	5	12	19	26	7

The square contains all the values. A is always 1 and N is always 14. To generate the values of say, the 7-gematria, read from (7) as follows: B= 16, C= 5 etc., up to M= 25, then return by the lower row, so that O= 3, P= 18 etc., back to Z= 12. The gematrias of 15–25 employ the reverse orders; for instance, for the 19-gematria, B= 12, C= 23 up to M= 3, then O= 25, P= 10 back to Z= 16.

SOME CORRESPONDENCES FROM LIBER AL:

Firstly some correlations with Nuit:

NUIT	Value	Base #
Nuit, Zero, Thou, Thelema	64	1
Nuit, Zero, Thou, Fire	76	3
Nuit, Zero, Thou, Fire, Aiwaz	42	5
Nuit, Fire	72	7
Nuit, Thou, Beauty, Ecstasy, Pea	54	9
Nuit, Thee, Fire, Magick	78	11
Nuit, Thee, Fire, Us	34	15
Nuit, Thou, Tarot	58	17
Nuit, Fire, First	40	19
Nuit, Zero, Fire, Space, Women	70	21
Nuit, Zero, Thou, Fire	36	23
Nuit, Zero, Thou, Abyss, Woman	48	25

In the *Book of the Law*, Nuit is identified with 'zero', in 'that men speak not of thee as one but as none', and with the 'first' principle of the three chapters of the book. In the gematrias she is identified with woman, space and the emptiness of the abyss (cf 'to her the stooping starlight', *AL 1:16* and elsewhere) and seemingly, through the image of fire, with her priestess, the Scarlet Woman. Connections are made with Thelema and Aiwaz, and the occurrence of 'beauty', 'ecstasy' and 'peace' put one in mind of the promise in *AL 1:58* of 'Peace unutterable, rest, ecstasy' as does the connection with tarot the ownership of 'my book' (*AL 1:57*).

Now for the really interesting bit: take any of the paired gematrias and average their numbers (eg. 48 and 64 from gematrias 25 and 1) or take the overall mean and we get—wait for it—56. 'I am Nuit, and my word is six and fifty' (*AL 1:24*)—which it certainly is not in any of the single systems; the gematrias must be taken together to reveal this relationship, a method we have found useful in other instances.

This also demonstrates Nuit's identity with Isis: 'Isis' is one of the very few words we have examined whose number is the same in all twelve gematrias: it is 56.

BABALON	Value	Base #
Babalon, Force, Beast	47	1
Babalon, Power, Mystery, Pentagram, Kingdom	81	3
Babalon, Goddess, Mystery, Current, Kingdom	93	5
Babalon, Magic	61	7
Babalon, Red, Flame	49	9
Babalon, Goddess	65	11
Babalon, Current, Mystery, Creation	79	15
Babalon, Current, Mystery, Eleven, Kingdom	95	17
Babalon, Current, Kingdom	83	19
Babalon, Current	63	23
Babalon, Current	97	25

Taken together, the following exegesis may be developed: Babalon is the Malkuth aspect of Goddess, the Bride and the Kingdom, and source of the magical current, power, force or flame exemplified by the Angels of Malkuth, the Ashim or Souls of Fire through whose agency the mystery of creation is fulfilled in the Kingdom.

The correspondence matrix of Hadit is similarly one-pointed:

HADIT	Value	Base #
Hadit, Yesod, Aleph	52	3
Hadit, Yesod, Aleph, Lust	54	5
Hadit, Yesod, Because	66	7
Hadit, Yesod, Aleph, Lion	64	9
Hadit, Yesod, Aleph	58	11
Hadit, Aleph	56	15
Hadit, Aleph, Life, Star, Sex	50	17
Hadit, God, Word	48	19
Hadit, Aleph, Logos	60	21
Hadit, Aleph, Logos, Aiwass	62	23
Hadit, Yesod, Logos	72	25

Hadit is strongly identified with Yesod, the Foundation and seat of the generative energies, and with Aleph, the primal seed of activity emanating from Kether to Chokmah. Hadit is declared to be the point, and the fire of the stars in *AL 2:2* & *6*, and identity with life force or kundalini is made in *AL 2:6*—'I am life and the giver of life' and *2:22*—'I am the snake that giveth knowledge and delight and bright glory'. The 'word' and 'logos' correspondences are involved in a whole complex of cross-correlations between Hadit, Aiwass and Aiwaz which those interested may care to follow up.

The Hermit, as the highest magical grade of Thelema (*AL 1:40*) is specifically identified with sexual magic and the raising of Kundalini:

HERMIT	Value	Base #
Hermit, Orgasm, Goddess, Perfect, Union, Kingdom	73	1
Hermit, Supreme, Serpent	89	3
Hermit, Orgasm, Glory, Scorpio	87	5
Hermit, Universe, Holy Grail	101	7
Hermit, Kundalini, The Wise	109	11
Hermit, Orgasm, Deity, Unity, Whole	65	17
Hermit, Orgasm	67	19
Hermit, Orgasm	79	23

> *'For there are also of my friends who he hermits. Now think not to find them in the forest or on the mountain but in beds of purple, caressed by magnificent beasts of women with large limbs and masses of flaming hair about them' (AL 2:24).*

Another level of interrelatedness is perceived, however, when the following table is compared:

SERPENT	Value	Base #
Serpent, Supreme, Brilliant	97	1
Serpent, Supreme, Hermit	89	3
Serpent, Supreme	77	5
Serpent, Supreme	109	7
Serpent, Supreme	95	9
Serpent, Supreme	131	11
Serpent, Supreme, Union, Force, Pentagram	65	15
Serpent, Supreme	101	17
Serpent, Supreme, Horus, Divine	87	19
Serpent, Supreme	119	21
Serpent, Supreme	107	23
Serpent, Supreme	99	25

All the underlined numbers are identical with underlined numbers in the Hermit table. This is another way in which the twelve systems interpenetrate, generating multi-level correspondences. A quite different form of correspondence can be seen with the values of Hoor-paar-kraat:

GEMATRIA No.	VALUE	FACTORISED VALUE
17, 21	91	7x13
5, 11, 19, 25	117	9x13
1, 7, 15, 21	143	11x13
3, 9	169	13x13

They are all odd multiples of 13, and the key number which was used to decipher the *Qabalah of AL*, 143, is present in four other gematrias but not in the 11-gematria itself, just as the Lord of Silence is conspicuous in his absence from *AL*. He left, however, a highly organised numerical structure intimately related to the elucidation of the book.

Finally, another style of correlation sheds light on *AI 2:27*, where Hadit warns of the dangers of the magical path; 'There is great danger in me, for who doth not understand the runes shall make a great miss. He shall fall down into the pit called Because and there he shall perish with the dogs of Reason.' In the 11-gematria the phrase 'there is great danger in me' adds up to 333, the number of Choronzon, demon of the Abyss. Examination of the correspondences of 'because' details some of the conceptual traps that have claimed many an unwary adept:

BECAUSE	Value	IN BASE #
Because, Will	56	1
Because, Baphomet, Adrift	84	3
Because, Desire	74	5
Because, Hadit (!)	66	7
Because, Love (!)	50	9
Because, Lust, Secret, Magick (!)	64	15
Because, Initiation	86	23

'For there is a factor infinite and unknown, and all their words are skew-wise'.

None of these correspondences show up in the 11-gematria; neither does the following investigation of the 'dogs of reason'; 'reason' is linked with 'chains' in gematrias 1, 3, 7, 9, 17, 19, 13 and 25, warning us clearly of the restrictive action of the lower mind when it interferes with the magical process.

However we are vouchsafed a deeper insight into the identity of these canine servitors of Choronzon by gematria 5, in which 'reason' is linked to 'Pluto'. Presumably at least one of them is the beloved Walt Disney character in a new and sinister guise.

We hope that this article may have opened up a whole new field of enquiry and that others will be stimulated to further explore multi-valued gematria. To this end we are offering our source work 'The Dictionary of English Gematria'. This incorporates a base of over 600 selected words taken through each of the 12 gematrias and indexed both by alphabet and number.

AZODAI Stele

This was an exploratory collage of other drawings, playing around and letting new forms emerge. Early on in my magical career, I came across the words of William Blake: 'I must create my own system or be enslaved by another man's.' I was groping towards a scheme of magic that didn't yet exist for me, something that felt like it was grounded in my own weird experiences, a synthesis of magical identity with remembered embodied energy-events from my psychedelic days, overlaid with the ideas of Wilhelm Reich I'd read about back then.

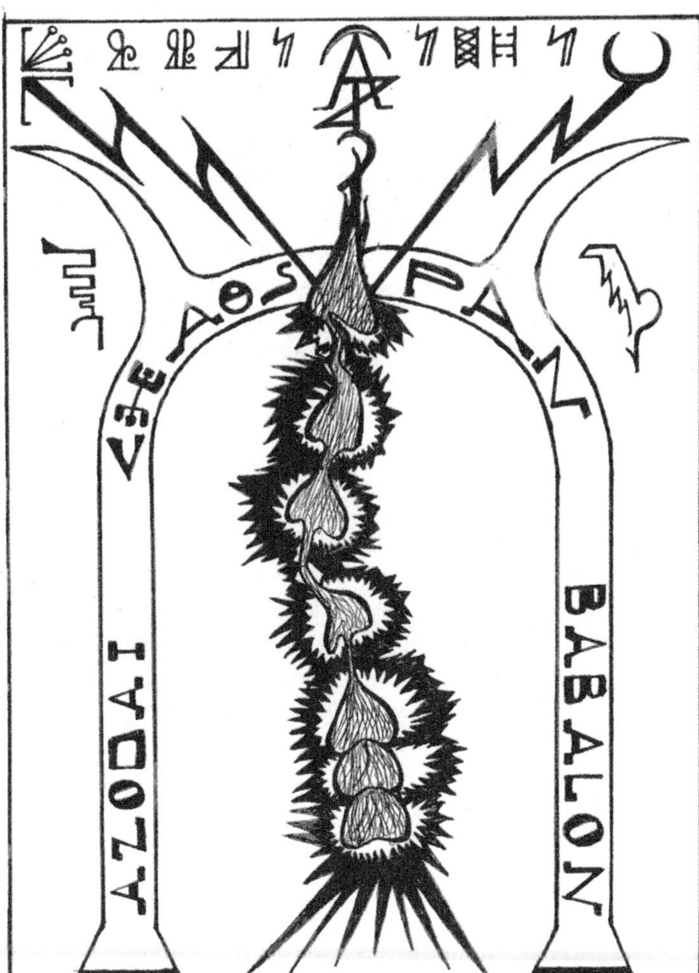

Pagan News

I lived in Leeds for twenty years, 1976–96, and it was where I became a full-time magician. By that, I mean I accepted that I wanted to, and was able to, live my days magically; spending much of my time doing magic, studying it, discussing it with other wonderfully weird people and beginning to write about it. I made enough money to get by, and gaining more would have conflicted with living my most interesting life.

I remember the 1980s–90s as being full of exciting magical experiments and discussions, and also the shadow of 'satanic panic'. Wild accusations were made and children taken from their parents on little or no evidence. Various pagan organizations and groups, including the Sorcerer's Apprentice, were working to get some truth out there, to shine a light on the imaginative excesses of Christian social workers.

There was of course a whole media circus around it. One figure who managed to get his face on the TV a few times was a Lancashire preacher called Kevin Logan (known to us, naturally, as Kev the Rev). This gentleman would spout off about how bad magic and paganism were, and eventually we got a chance to answer back, on a documentary series called Open Space which ran a film called *Lucifer Over Lancashire* in 1987 (utilizing of course The Fall's song of that name). We told the team who contacted us that we'd do a special event for them to film, up at the dramatic-looking Brimham Rocks on Ilkley Moor. We met the crew at Ray Sherwin's and walked up to the moor top in the dark. I walked beside a cameraman who kept complaining about the job. Thinking maybe he was used to easier working conditions, I asked him, 'Where do you normally work?' Glumly, he answered, 'Beirut'. It's easy to forget how readily some people are spooked by even just talking about the occult, which was all he'd been exposed to at that stage.

Up at the rocky outcrop, with a large fire lit, the director was happy. 'It's like a Goya for the '80s', he declared. Our working involved quite a bit of drumming and chanting, then the banner we'd made getting burned. The banner carried a sigil against US nuclear arms in Britain.[5]

In 1989, I took over the essential oils business Id Aromatics from Ray Sherwin and his business partner, and started to make a living doing something I really enjoyed. I've always loved aromatics and can still remember the first time I smelled frankincense in a church, and the first time I smelled some essential oils a friend had brought back from a festival. This career move meant my partner and I did some travelling, excused on business

[5] 1987, March 30th BBC2. *Lucifer over Lancashire*. Director: Paul Pawlikowski, Open Space, BBC2.

grounds to source rare ingredients such as aloeswood oil. The following piece was published in an issue of Pagan News from that time. It seems a tad stylized and over-written to me now.

Note: Phil Hine won an award for his use of the newish technology DTP to produce that zine, *Pagan News.* PN was a unique forum for all sorts of occult, Thelemic, pagan, chaoist and other people, and it ran for some years. The most substantial item I wrote for PN was a rather anti-New Age piece called 'Moronic Interference', which isn't in this collection because it is to be published in Phil Hine and Rodney Orpheus's forthcoming collection of PN articles.[6]

[6] Phil Hine and Rodney Orpheus's forthcoming collection of Pagan News articles: no release date at time of writing.

LETTER FROM EGYPT *BY SESOSTRIS*

South of the Aswan Dam, the desert road is arrow-straight, front and aft to each horizon. The sun is just up; on the left, each sand grain makes its own shadow, turning the whole land black, and on the right the grains scatter back a soft orange. Low hills appear, conical black mounds of broken rock like slagheaps. This is Gaia the Hag's Chaos Theme Park. The ground heats up, and distant hills float above the heat-haze. Two rock formations like crumbling sphinxes face each other over a gulf of sand.

At Abu Simbel, the two temples are monuments to the astonishing but highly tasteful egomania of Ramses II. We'd long run out of superlatives. The Hathor temple of Nefertiti celebrates Goddess in quite a different mood to the inhuman beauty of the desert. Here, she is all pleasure and love and music. The two aspects are two gigantic tendencies in human desire: on the one hand, for the embeddedness of the voluptuary in layer upon layer of rich and subtle sensation, and on the other, for the untrammelled freedom of deserts or outer space, away from the constraints of physical habit or even comfort.

The car didn't seem up to getting us back across the surface of Mars, which gave us the opportunity to test out a pre-constructed general-purpose elemental Servitor. A passing mechanic stopped by. We paid our respects to Horus and Sebek at Kom Ombu.

The Karnak complex of temples near Luxor must be a geomant's dream; growing out from the vast Hypostyle Hall, the world's largest temple, are numerous shrines. temples. pylons, with an apparent overall plan. Two avenues of Sphinxes run out from the Temple, one of which ran 5 km to the Temple at Luxor. Each end is still visible, with a chunk of modem city in between.

Ten years ago, I'd taken the magical name of Sesostris for a series of workings, and after a day wandering about, we decided to take a look at the Sesostris chapel. This turned out to be closed, but a guard motioned us over to a small temple on the edge of the complex. There was a courtyard, and two locked shrines leading off. For some small backsheesh, we were let into the left-hand door. The Shrine contained a two-metre Ptah figure, with the face completely smashed, wreathed in a cloud of sweet, Sudanese incense. The second shrine had incense too, and a massive Sekhmet of black granite, in perfect condition. Each shrine was open to the sky via a small rectangular hole. One of the guards, 'for luck', and presumably for his own voyeuristic purpose, had each of us touch Sekhmet's lips, breast and belly and then place both our hands together on Her face, and kiss.

On the west of the river, across from Luxor, is West Thebes, the physical Amenta of the Pharaohs, their special Land of Death. Against a backdrop of stark cliffs is set the Mortuary Temple of Hatshepsut, the female Pharaoh who ruled with the false beard of Pharaonic office. Quite 20th century in appearance, this cool and elegant sanctuary was built by Senmut, her architect and almost certainly her lover. The guard took us for a scramble up the cliff-base scree to a concealed tomb in the rock, telling us that it was Senmut's. Its small size made this seem unlikely. On the walls were two pictograms, marked with archeologist's numbers. In one of these a stylized man and woman couple from the rear; the guard pointed and said, 'Hatshepsut and Senmut'.

Down on the plains towards the river stands yet another monument to Ramses II, the Ramesseum. Together with the giant statues there are the usual pictures of ol' Ramesses doing a great deal of smiting, usually of Libyans. George Bush would approve, and his first language obviously isn't English, either.

In terms of magical energetics, the tomb of Queen Tausert, usurped by Set-Nakht, is the place in the Valley of the Kings. The walls of the empty burial chamber are covered in weirdly untypical gods: a winged ram dominates one wall, stars are everywhere. After a few minutes, we both noticed a loud ringing in the ears, rising to an oceanic roar at the threshold of audial hallucination. The guard leaned quietly against the wall; I tried to wonder what six hours a day of this would do to him.

Cairo had warmed up to mild-wintry when we got back. One day in the Egyptian Museum is not long enough to do more than skim and occasionally pounce on something. Looking for some kind of visual handle on Predynastic Egypt, we found a small slate palette, apparently used for grinding green eyeshadow. This star-limbed Goddess (see illustration) is a product of the El Badari culture, at least 4500 BCE. Sections of the Museum are permanently closed to the general public, as is normal in museums. However, across one of the public galleries, crudely closed with chairs and stuff, we spotted what must have been the Stele of Revealing. Maybe some zealous Fundamentalist Thelemites had been frightening the tourists off, and the staff had closed it for a while. For the curious, the catalogue number was 3364, in U22.

We rounded off our Cairo stay at the New Arizona belly-dancing club. Through the seedy doorway into the aroma of best frankincense, our kind host Hassan assured us proudly that this was the cheapest, and best, such club in town. We sat in a quiet corner, and the four-piece band struck up, the in-house singer switching in an echo unit which made his voice resemble the shattered electric Koranics of the muezzins. A guest Lebanese singer sang songs of the sorrows of the war in eerie quarter-tones.

The third dancer really had the front tables going when one of the men from a table of boozy Saudis jumped up on stage and started dancing. This was too much for her manager, who was minding the tips-box at the back of the stage. He hit some treble discords on the piano, then slammed the lid down. Total Silence. A giant who would be recognisable as a bouncer anywhere in the world joined the manager at the young Saudi's table. Someone said something which was clearly very funny, which restored the good atmosphere, but Hassan had missed it, so we didn't get a translation. Throughout the night, during or in between acts, the members of the audience would get up and hand tips to the singer or MC on stage. These were usually followed by a salutation to some other person or group in the room. This is a great way to get to know who's in the place. The drunk in front of us seemed to like the lads from Saudia Airlines, and we learned to our amusement that the fat man dripping gold and having a serious relationship with a bottle of Johnny Walker at the next table was a local judge.

Hassan had said that we must stay for another act, and it was well worth it. The band were from the Institute of Arab Music, and played this powerful, pacy music with a dark and solemn undertow, while the very best dancers danced. It was a total Hathor invocation, as far as I was concerned. At the end, I stumbled out to the toilet, to find the attendant on his knees, up to his elbows in Polyfilla, fixing the sink.

Oxford Thelemic Symposium 1989

This annual event was held in Oxford town hall's main chamber, with its splendid Zodiacal ceiling, and ran regularly from 1986 until at least the mid-'90s, then sporadically after that. In those early years we used to go down as a party from Leeds, usually on a coach trip. One year two friends suggested we split a car hire, so they reserved a Sierra for the weekend. On the day, the salespeople at the car hire place were very apologetic—the Sierra wasn't available. But for the same price, would we mind taking this silver-grey Mercedes? So we arrived in Oxford in style, Laibach blasting out on the shiny new CD player, which was good going, considering we couldn't even afford a pizza each in—what was to us—the shockingly expensive town centre.

Other people came from miles away too. It was a major social event of the magical calendar, in those days before even email, in no small part due to the friendly after-parties.

Until I re-read my Thelemic Symposium review I'd forgotten that I was for a while the Reviews Editor of *Pagan News*.

REVIEW OF THE OXFORD THELEMIC SYMPOSIUM

The third national Symposium of Thelemic Magick was held at Oxford's Town Hall, on Saturday the 22nd of October [1989]. The event took place in the council chamber, which is ringed with the signs of the zodiac.

Ken Cox of the Typhonian OTO took the podium first, giving an excellent talk on the magick of Surrealism. Ken presented a wide overview of Surrealist ideas, and demonstrated the 'random' method of decalcomania (ink or gouache on folded paper) as a means of constructing sigils and obsessional images.

Lionel Snell completed the morning's events with one of his extraordinary, intricate talks. Taking as a starting point the astrology of Uranus in the change of Aeons, he traced the assimilation of the ideas of both Aleister Crowley and Austin Osman Spare (along with those of Einstein for more general comparison) from 1904 to the complete Uranian cycle to 1988. This pathway spawned more ideas than there's space to mention. For more of Lionel's thoughts have a look at his new book *Words Made Flesh*.

In order to fit in lunch I had to miss the next item on the day's agenda. Andrew Collins, author of *The Black Alchemist* gave a talk on his 'psychic quest', which involved the channeling of Crowley. I returned to catch a workshop on Kali by Mike Magee and Andrew Stenson (both members of the tantrik order, AMOOKOS[7]). They provided a whole host of Kali-attributes and ideas, which led into the day's liveliest discussion.

The final sit-down event was Mike Goss's showing of the 'Magic Lantern' cycle of films by Kenneth Anger. Unfortunately, the video quality was rather poor. Mike also ran an excellent disco (with slides) at the evening social.

My overall impression of the Symposium was lots of energy but virtually no arguments. It was certainly an improvement on the near drongoism of last year's afternoon session. Perhaps a little more discussion might have been fruitful. Still, an excellent event, with a great opportunity to make contacts.

---

[7] The Arcane Magical Order of the Knights of Shambhala.

Chaos International

After the breakup of the so-called 'Circle of Chaos' in 1987–88 I retired from involvement in groups for a while. I came back to active engagement with the IOT in 1991, at the world meeting in Burg Lockenhaus, Austria. I was just in time to see Pete Carroll retire from the IOT.

Chaos International magazine crystallized out of the IOT scene over those years. I suggested the name because it had to have 'chaos' in it and sound sophisticated, and my girlfriend was reading *Harpers and Queen International*. The first issue was in 1986, edited by PD Brown and Ray Sherwin. Editorship changed by design over the next few issues, edited by myself, then Phil Hine, then finally settling down with Ian Read from issue 6 through to issue 23 (and beyond).

My editorship lasted for two issues. I was tremendously excited at this opportunity to publish something which would be part of this new current, but it had to be classy, and all I had was a decidedly cranky old mechanical typewriter that had survived a domestic fire, so half its casing was melted. I needed something better, at the very least a better typewriter. Before I even got round to doing a spell I got a surprise gift: my uncle, who always sent me a small sum of money, say £10–20 to have fun on my birthday, sent me £100 out of the blue. I bought an electric typewriter, which seemed the absolute pinnacle of publishing sophistication. I looked at the previous two issues and started thinking about what I wanted my issues to look like. I realised that I needed a typeface a little smaller than the typewriter delivered, so I typed up a few passages and went to experiment on a photocopier. I used the one in Leeds University Students' Union, just up the road from my flat on Bellevue Road. In those days, photocopiers came with a 'Reduction' function, useful for matching up the sizes of text objects. I eventually settled on a reduction to 80% of the typewriter output.

This meant I had to buy some A3 paper, cut it down to the size I needed, just the right amount larger than A4 to give an A4 page with an 80% reduction, and type up all the articles destined for CI. I then took the outsized pages to the photocopier and reduced them to their final size of A4. I don't ever remember resenting this labour, because it was one of love.

From Issue 1: Magical Aeonics

This was my first lengthy published magical piece. I'd been trying to work out what I wanted to say about magic, and had pinned a large piece of paper to the wall forming a sprawling mind-map of all my obsessions and the links between them, teasing out usable ideas in the spaces between magic, politic(k)s and what later became known as occulture. Eventually I distilled it into this piece, which was an attempt to answer my own big question: *Why does magic to change the world so seldom succeed?*

The concept I chose to pin all this on was Aeonics. In the 36 years since I wrote this, we magicians have decolonized our language quite a bit and the whole idea of Aeons has started to look a whole lot less believable. As a result, the following article needs a good deal more reappraisal than most of the pieces included in this book.

The idea of Aeons, as I write about them below, stems from Crowley's three concepts—Isis, an Aeon of Nature; Osiris, an Aeon of the Dying God ; and Horus, the new Aeon whose Prophet Crowley declared himself to be. The model I use is in turn based on Pete Carroll's five-Aeon model—see 'The Chart' in the article.

These esoteric theories of history are based on the idea of progress, that one interpretation of reality follows on historically from another. Progress is such a tempting idea; in 1992 I created a sound-piece, *The Galafron Rite*,[8] which was basically a pathworking that took the listener through four Aeons and onto the cusp of the fifth. It was tremendously idealistic, imagining a process of liberation of thought which would overcome the horrors of the previous four Aeons. I remember one passionate response to it, the listener saying they wished we could frog-march all the Aeonic laggards, those religious folks and Scientism devotees, through the Galafron Rite and bring them up to our exalted present state! Such an attitude arises from a kind of memetic chauvinism—'our ideas are better for everyone, not just for us'. You can see how this could become quite a problem.

Another model which is obviously related to Aeonics (but whose authors would no doubt strenuously deny such a connection) is the Spiral Dynamics model, which mystical philosopher Ken Wilber incorporated into his Integralism metatheory. To cut a long story short, rather than five Aeons this model has upwards of nine 'memes', and counting. The memes have numbers and colours. Some of the memes line up well with Carroll's Aeons: meme 2, 'Purple' is close to 'Shamanism'; memes 3 and 4, 'Red' and 'Amber', comprise 'Paganism'; Meme 5, 'Orange', is identical to 'Modernism/Atheism'.

---

[8] Lee D, et al. (1992). *The Galafron Rite & Timedragons: An Astral Working of Illumination.*

We begin to glimpse the underlying ideology: Wilber's use of Spiral Dynamics is explicitly in the service of integrating ideas from different academic disciplines with mystical concepts, East with West and so on, and thereby promoting a new kind of faith in progress. However, his notion of progress shows up in his treatment of Meme 2, 'Purple': he positions it to be about people living in a magical, shamanistic world, but dismisses the magic of that world as primitive superstition. We see clearly the dead hand of colonialism applied to an Aeonic model.

Of course, the fact of the matter is that you can make up any damn Aeonic sequence that suits your ideological goals. Psychedelic thinker Terrence McKenna tells us it all started when we emerged from the forest, ate psilocybin mushrooms and acquired language. In the early 20th Century, Traditionalist writer Julius Evola made up a sequence of prehistoric cultural transitions that supported his (unfortunately influential) ultra-masculine warrior fantasy world. So take your pick, magician, and choose carefully!

Bearing this in mind, a more useful approach to Aeonics is that written about by Alistair Livingstone back in the 1980s. His own magical current was that of Ma'at, another Aeonic figure in the post-Crowley Thelemic landscape, and Ma'at was always a gnosis more popular than Horus with the psychedelic fraternity, emphasizing Truth and Justice, things we so long for in these times. The Ma'at Aeon was channeled by various magicians whose thinking soon left Crowley behind and detached that Aeon from any principle of linear history: the Aeon of Ma'at was something you worked while still embedded in the historical Aeon of Horus. Livingstone took this further in his observation that all the different Aeonic value-systems are living side by side in the contemporary city: on one side, my neighbour may be a Muslim, on another an Atheist, on another a mad hippy ecstatic.[9] He referred to this model of Aeonics as having more in common with the geological concept of plate tectonics than that of history. In this model, Aeons become recognizable gestalts made up of cultural tendencies, but we don't have to shoehorn them into a hierarchy, nor do we have to claim that our favoured Aeon is right for everyone. This decouples Aeonics from Progress.

---

[9] In an article or letter I cannot find.

MAGICAL AEONICS

INTRODUCTION

Aeonics is a way of looking at the inner levels of history, of connecting our knowledge of the past external to inner layers of myth. Each of us has an individual history, stored in memory, which distinguishes us from others. We also partake of, and are immersed in, ideas, ideals and struggles common to our entire culture, or even species. These elements of myth, these archetypes, are not static, immutable forms but change in ways corresponding to outer history.

Aeonics is the study of these changes, a magical awareness of the shifts in mass consciousness that generate the succession (or coexistence) of aeons. That aeons can coexist is implied in the Gnostic definition of the word. In brief, the Gnostic cosmogonies had these features: an unspeakable central mystery, apprehended only through gnosis, or direct altered perception, which fragments itself and gives rise to a number of spiritual principles, or aeons, which further devolve into the patterns of the material world. These aeons may be thought of as similar to the thirty Aethyrs of John Dee's magic, and are closely related to the Gnostic concept of Archons, which roughly translates as Great Old Ones.

To sort through past and present myths to catch a glimpse of these principles is a tricky and endless task, rather like digging in quicksand. From a magical point of view, why bother? The answer is concerned with the nature of the resistance encountered in magical action. The process of initiation consists in a large part of sorting through automatic responses programmed by personal history and stripping away those that are superfluous to our chosen desires. Up to a point this may satisfy us, to clear the way to expressing our individual wills and get on with doing them. Beyond that elusive point, however, we require understanding of the nature and strength of the resistance that confronts us.

It is a truism in magic that, in principle, everything is possible, but that in practice some things are not. This is symbolized by some magicians as the Sphere of Availability, a zone of magical possibilities which is extended by each subsequent success. Initially, one overcomes fairly superficial patterns of habit, of negative thought and inner dialogue by reprogramming one's self-image. A simple example is positive thinking: one gets better and better every day, challenging more and more of one's negative assumptions. Until, that is, one comes up against more deeply ingrained prejudices and limitations. Many people reach a stage adequate for their desires before this point is reached, and more or less happily accept their limitations. Others, finding their dissatisfaction to be more deeply rooted, go on to challenge these deeper prejudices, and become magicians. There is no clearly-drawn line between the personal and the transpersonal in this process (the process itself may well occur 'back-to-front', the deeper dissatisfactions having to be come to terms with before the magician is able to focus on mundane desires, giving an impression of 'descending from spirit to matter'). However, at some stage the magician encounters resistances which appear to stem from 'outside' himself. Being acquainted with paradox, he knows they are 'inside' as well, but further, that they are not unique or personal to him.

These resistances are forms, solidified ideas, left over from previous cycles of action. Not the magician's, but those who went before him. In the guises of gods, philosophies, codes of morality, institutions, they are the demonic shells left behind by the used-up creative energies of another era. They may be very powerful, but their power derives from inertia: internally, from inertia of belief caused by apathy or fear of the new; externally by the inertias of their physical habits (more on this later).

Magic has its own inertias and institutions. We must build by using what went before, but in our present position we have the pick of the aeons. We can learn from, and use, any magics of the past. Hopefully, we can discard the dross, assimilate the essentials, and rework them along lines that will nourish and vitalize ourselves and the world. We are creating the new, or suffocating under the weight of the old, with a speed and fluidity unique in history. In this Kali Yuga, our systems are disposable: if you can't make it fit, don't wear it.

This article is a personal exploration of themes from the past and presented in an attempt to steal a glance at the growing edge of contemporary magic.

THE CHART

This is divided into three sections: the *centre block*, containing nearly everything, is a non-exhaustive (and personal) summary of where our dominant magical themes have come from. These are some of the traditions we have records of, and therefore historical access to.

The *upper section* represents the Shamanic Aeon, which stretches through prehistoric time back to the earliest humans. It is the ultimate source of all magic. Anthropologists characterize this level as *participation mystique,* representing in the individual the state of childlike merging of 'magic' and 'reality', of passion and belief. Lao Tzu, looking back to the Golden Age, refers to the 'uncarved block'. This is the closest human condition to the source energies of Chaos. In a Shamanic culture, the forces of nature are seen as non-human-hearted; the idols tend to be atavisms: birds, snakes, foxes and so forth. Humans are seen as inextricably and necessarily part of the web of organic beings, utterly dependent on the well-being of the tribe and the whole ecology. The social level corresponds largely to hunter-gatherer societies.

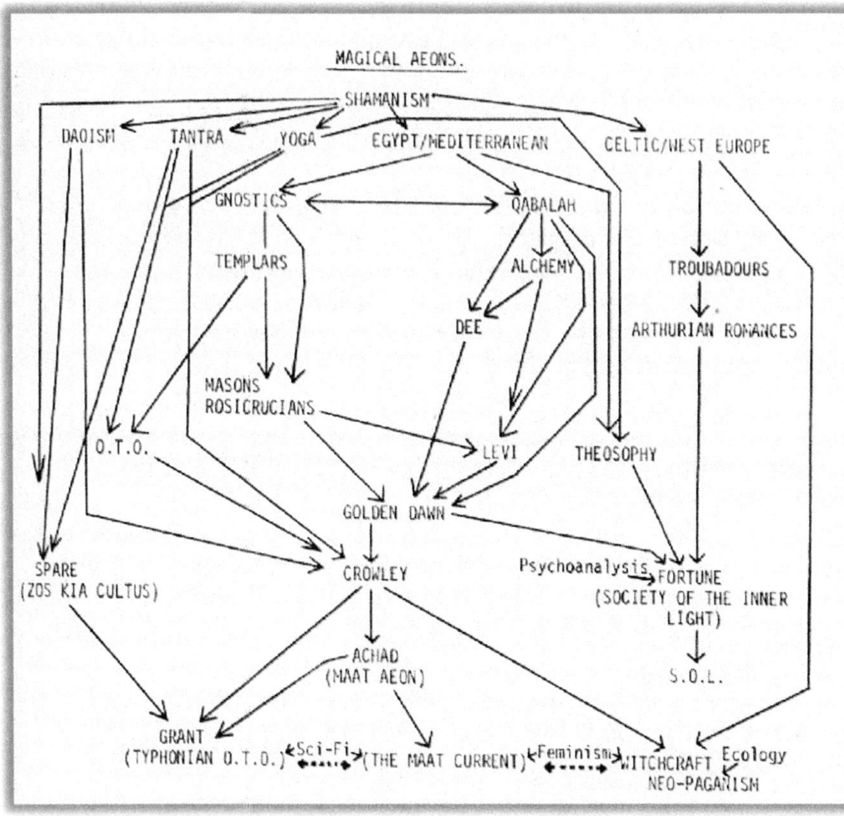

The middle block, or historical time-zone, may be subdivided (courtesy of Pete Carroll) into three Aeons. The *Second*, or *Pagan Aeon* is associated with settled agriculture and cities. Humans live, by our standards, close to nature, but material sophistication and individual interest have begun to increase. Multiple humanoid deities reflect the whole range of human desires and passions. At some stage in this process, the patriarchal warrior cults emerge: the child-ego is trying to make sense of the world in terms of human conflict. The myths are filled with heroes, who fight against monsters and titans left unkilled or unchained from a previous Aeon or, when these are not available, against each other. Nature having been partially mastered for agriculture, the main theme is the succession of families and dynasties who control these resources. The forces of nature are grafted uncomfortably onto the all-too-human gods, who wield them arbitrarily unless placated with sacrifices. The later patriarchal stages of paganism correspond to the early stages of Crowley's Aeon of Osiris and the dying gods.

The process of centralization of power into state institutions and the consolidation of patriarchy are achieved in the *Third or Monotheistic Aeon*. The single God is made in the image of authority in relation to the ideal citizen, tame and repressed, and ready to die for deity or empire. Rigid suppression of whole sections of society, particularly women, and the anathematization of female sexuality are main themes of the full-blown Piscean Age societies.

The *Fourth or Atheistic Aeon* corresponds to the rise of superstates, capitalism, and revolutionary foment. Its symbols include the Death of God, and the rise of a scientific priesthood. The citizen is no longer reflected (however shabbily) in a deity, and is no longer trusted. Insane intricacies of bureaucracy, mass paranoia and insecurity and secret police forces all abound. Distrust of other people accelerates with population density. The planet has become a lump of dead matter to be plundered in the name of an economic growth which benefits few. Powerful weapons are bought and sold in vast quantities. Violence erupts everywhere. As complex societies threaten to disintegrate into warring 'terrorist' factions, and millions crack under the pressure, new ideas are being born. The confusion of late-Atheistic society is the crucible which melts down old patterns and allows us to cast new ones. This corresponds to Crowley's Aeon of Horus, the God of War and vengeance who purges the old Aeon.

We may have centuries more of World War Three ahead, but a new Aeon is forming now; our magics are the core energies of its formation. The rest of this article is an attempt to place markers on the lower dotted line of the diagram, to glimpse themes which are emerging facets of the new magic, starting from recent *non*-magical influences, and working towards the present day.

FROM PSYCHOANALYSIS TO OPEN-ENDED THERAPIES

Psychoanalysis succeeded in secularizing the sense of sin. Previously, mental disorders were seen largely as punishment, often for specific sins such as masturbation. The early psychoanalysts were caught up in the emergence of Atheistic society, and it was to that society that their work tried to restore people. The wedge that religion had driven between the human animal and the social human had been removed, but the split persisted.

Later psychotherapies shifted the emphasis to what Jung called 'individuation', raising up the entire human abilities to full functioning. Reich realised the explosive political potential of psychic energies, Maslow utilized 'peak experiences' (what a magician would call gnosis) in the sufferer to transform the self-image. Psychotherapy converged, in its rediscovery of human potentials, with magic, which borrowed numerous terms from its junior partner. The revival of magic has now reached a point where the influence of psychotherapy has waned; the flow is in the other direction, towards Jungian Tarot groups, and ritualized group work, for instance.

FROM NEW SCIENCE TO SCI-FI

This influence is of a different order to the last; the emergence of a workable new physics, with its observer-dependent universe, its wave-particle paradox and its principled uncertainty has replaced the rigid clockwork universe of the old physics with a universe where magic seems much more likely. In the wake of theories such as energy-less information transfer, even physicists are speculating profound connections between consciousness and the 'physical' world. Our degree of conscious involvement with the universe has begun to transform it from an assemblage of dead matter to a semi-living network of energies.

The increasingly bizarre terminology of physics has been borrowed by both science fiction and magic. Our most popular modern myth-form, sci-fi takes us into speculations ranging from terminal destruction through to utopias involving life-extension, genetic engineering, space travel and expanded mental faculties.

This latter is the growing edge of the science-magic interaction; whilst the influence of physical theories on magic has probably peaked, the scientists are stumbling into the 'etheric' zones of magic itself. The vested interests of controllers make sure that the new work is secret, and ostensibly discredited if any emerges. It seems unlikely that there are no secret laboratories working on telepathy, telekinesis and remote sensing already. This gives an urgency to open magical research: the only defence of individuals against psi-weaponry and psi-control is their own magical training.

ECOLOGY

The impact of ecology is related both to science and to the inner levels of sexual politics. The dominant worldview is alienated, patriarchal and materially rapacious. A broad radical opposition to this rapacity is forming, manifesting in ways such as Greenpeace and the camps at nuclear weapons bases. The political philosophy is underpinned by the Gaia Hypothesis: that the planet is better understood, and therefore cared for, if it is considered as a unified system, a part-organic being with its own homeostatic and defence mechanisms and, in a sense, its own evolution which intersects with ours. Devotion to Gaia is becoming a cornerstone of much of the new politics, and this crosses over into magic. She is a vast, mysterious being whose secrets we have literally only scratched the surface of. Organic beings have bodies made from Her substance, living on Her surface in a delicate equilibrium. Devotion to Gaia is surely more satisfying than devotion to the petty humanoid gods of past Aeons.

SEXUAL MAGIC AND SEXUAL POLITICS

The harnessing of sexual energies for magical purposes extends back to the Shamanic Aeon. Many ancient cultures represented their Gods and Goddesses with prominent sex-organs, especially in the Pagan Aeon, when human copulation was ritually associated with the fertility of crops and herd animals.

With the rise of patriarchies and the eclipse of the political power of women, we see the emergence of the possession of women by men as objects of sex and childbearing. With the full-blown patriarchies of the Monotheistic Aeon came sexual guilt and sin. The great religions have always recognized the power of sexual repression to infuse with energy their power-mad deities, and to keep the masses docile.

The turning point is reached with Atheism. 19th century atheist thinkers were tormented by the 'problem' of sexual ethics. With their childhood-engendered guilt complexes, and the opposition of society, they could only go so far in their removal of taboos. The next stage was the emergence of modern sexual magic, and the discovery of spiritual principles which are positive towards sexuality. The liberation of sex is not politically neutral; the release of the pent-up anarchic energies of sexuality acts like a depth-charge, shattering the belief-systems that its repression supported, and the received reality-view crumbles.

The most influential writer on sexual magic was no doubt Aleister Crowley. His *Book of the Law* says (I.51): 'Take your fill and will, when, where and with whom you will', adding 'But always unto me'. The speaker is Nuit, declaring the holiness of sex, and the method of experiencing that holiness (I.58): 'I give unimaginable joys on earth: certainty, not faith, while in life, upon death, peace unutterable, rest, ecstasy, nor do I demand aught in sacrifice'. The Gods are dead, and a new Goddess is arisen, who requires neither the passions nor the intellect to be negated. No sacrifice, no striving for an abstract faith, but the ecstasy of love and life, here and now.

Crowley's personality paid dearly for his egress from respectability, his direct opposition to the hypocrisy of the time. In contrast, Dion Fortune wrote a good deal on occult sexuality, but never quite entered the new Aeon. Her writings, with few (and great) exceptions, are tainted with a bourgeois-Christian sense of security. The anarchic side of sexuality is paid lip-service to, in the form of Pan, frightening god of nature and lust, but his reign is temporary, confined to occult Mills-and-Boon-style interludes in Fortune's world of great houses and gymkhanas. Reading her advice on sexuality for occultists, it is obvious that respectability comes first. A worse example still of the taint of Christian sexual fear is found in the writings of CS Lewis. In his otherwise excellent *Silent Planet* trilogy, sex is treated as OK for lesser mortals (as long as they're married); the hero's heroism seems to be predicated on his impotence, a typical male Saviour figure. Lewis cannot hide his aversion to female sexuality; he clothes his anima in vague notions of sexual holiness, but the patriarchal virgin/whore duality glares through.

The subject of sexual freedom in itself, whilst still discussed by religious bigots, is a near-dead issue. Most people do much as they please sexually in modern Western societies. The growing edge of the discourse has turned since the Swinging Sixties towards the political dimensions of sexuality, and, on the magical scene, towards a reappraisal of sexual magic in the light of the politics of sex. No doubt the two main issues here are female liberation and the recognition of homo- and bi-sexuality as magically valid.

The influence on magic of the emergence of a new female consciousness is so profound, and developing so fast, that I can only touch upon it here. The breakdown of Christianity and the crisis of patriarchal techno-atheism has brought with it a weakening of the philosophy of patriarchy. The older political movements for the emancipation of women had as their aim the 'equality' of women in a male society. This was the beginning, a scratch on the surface and perhaps a summoning of courage towards a total assault on the anathematization of female sexuality, which underlies monotheistic culture. A great many women are developing a new articulation of female consciousness, re-working language itself to express non-male insights into self and society. Unless our social awareness can evolve to accommodate these insights, it is unlikely that society will survive, and unless the male magician pursues a dialogue at every level with female magicians it is unlikely he will have the privilege of co-creating the new Aeon, but instead will be left behind with the dross of the old. Let it be said, however, that it is a co-creation that is needed if society is not simply to re-enact the ancient swings between matriarchy and patriarchy. The other option of sexual separatism is obviously unlikely ever to become a majority movement.

Another radical counterpoint is provided by the issue of homosexuality in magic. One of magic's central themes is identity, where it comes from and how to develop it, transform it and shift its emphasis. One's identity is strongly tied up with one's sexuality, and the objects of one's sexual desire. All humans are potentially or actually bisexual, and exclusive heterosexuality, whilst it may well be a considered and happy free choice, generally has its roots in childhood conditioning. The parents note what the child has between its legs, and condition it accordingly, a conditioning the resulting adult may well find irksome or painful, especially since the same conditioning may have impacted the parents' own doubts about their heterosexuality. And so the dismal cycle of sexual misidentification and disaffection will continue down the generations until broken and opened up by a conscious free choice, and the bearing of the responsibility of that choice by elimination of guilt.

Occultists of rigid persuasions are still arguing about the nature of the 'energies' involved in homosexual magic. The more liberated magician is more likely to regard the energy of desire as essentially formless, and the form it is expressed in as the business solely of the consenting entities involved. This former type of misunderstanding gives rise to all kinds of demented bigotry, of which I quote a prize example from a contemporary occult magazine:

> *'...Homosexuals are not human... Genuine mature human beings cannot be anything but heterosexual, for such is their nature... the fact is that there are an increasing number of non-human 'Souls' occupying human bodies...as can clearly be seen from their auras. But I do not advise anyone to look at one, for it can damage the 'third eye' in a manner analogous to an arc-welder's flash damaging the physical one. I... suspect an attempt to exterminate, or at least emasculate, humanity... perhaps the aim is an easy genocide...'*

With 'occultists' like this, who needs Born Again Christians?

ANCESTORS, HIEROPHANTS AND ASCENDED MASTERS

> *'There is a word to say about the Hierophantic task....'- Liber AL, I.50*

There are a few, in fact. The Hierophant's task is to announce the Laws of the Aeon, the exoteric forms of the unspeakable inner changes. Rigidity, Fixed Earth, his mask has been that of a Pope during the last Aeons, the unreflective rock on which Church and State were built. Crowley changed the Hierophant Trump, and saw something 'sadistic' in the meaning of it, perhaps in the unswerving, almost cynical certitude of the mask. Crowley's Aeon of Horus was announced by Aiwass, much of whose exposition is holding up quite well in the Cowering Eighties, if you interpret it in certain ways.

The practice of the reception and interpretation of 'inspired utterances' has its roots in the Shamanistic and Pagan Aeons, in the practice of ancestor worship, the universal human tendency to ask advice of one's forebears, living or dead. This was revived in a debased form as Spiritualism in the last century, which consists, at best, of a mediated access to the unconscious intuition of the querent on minor family matters. Moving on from Spiritualism, the spectrum of communication takes in obscure symbolic utterances from personal 'guides', through the use of archetypal guide-figures in pathworking (where, hopefully, we are into magic proper, and the recipient understands that he or she is operating in a definite belief system), through to so-called Holy Books, purported to come from Ascended Masters.

This is a complex issue, where the usefulness of a communication may easily be outweighed by the interpreter's literal belief in the existence of the 'Higher Being' who delivered it, not to mention the time invested in decoding the obscure ideas involved. It is hard to see, for instance, why Theosophist Alice Bailey devoted thousands of pages to her Tibetans unless she really believed in them. This largely incomprehensible body of writings seems designed in its vastness, to keep readers' minds off any real magical work.

It is interesting to note, in this context, that the home of the 'Masters'[10] has moved in recent decades from the Himalayas to outer space. This suggests that if such documents have any validity, it is to be found in their ability to stretch the imagination, to train the mind to operate at the limits of its powers of conceptualization. One of the briefer, and therefore better, books of this kind is Dion Fortune's *The Cosmic Doctrine*, which states: 'The Masters as you picture them are all "imagination"...' and goes on to say: '...this is an endeavour to convey very abstract ideas in reasonably concrete form'. Whilst I find the very notion of 'Masters' offputting, the book certainly communicates a very deep and integrated gnostic state, which some may find valuable.

Thus the magician may use 'Holy Books' to train the subtler mental processes, but should be wary of identifying with the ideas in them. If we postulate an 'Aeonic Intelligence' existing behind the phenomena of time, then Aeonic/Hierophantic books are like snapshots of this Intelligence at a particular point in time. However accurate the snapshot is, however well-focused, the wave-crest of the Intelligence has already passed by, and the writings left behind become more and more of an empty shell as more time passes. The Aeonic Intelligence is in any case that of the magician himself, his own portion and facet of the race mind, and if he is to move beyond his limitations he must do so by a continual resort to his own inner truth. The outer Aeons are changing faster too, and magical ideas are programmed to self-destruct when obsolete, so that they don't add to the rubbish pile of the past. The magical survivor in this Kali Yuga is likely to be equipped with the wisdom of insecurity.

CHANGING VISIONS: EXTRATERRESTRIALS AND TIME-TRAVELLERS

> *'Another UFO By Royal Appointment:*
>
> *'An oval-shaped UFO has been spotted over Windsor Castle. The mystery craft flew close to the battlements in broad daylight. People watched in disbelief as the red, glowing machine—the size of a Mini—moved slowly across the sky.*

[10] HP Blavatsky, founder of the Theosophical Society, claimed her massively influential books were channelled (as we would say today) from 'Ascended Masters', highly evolved humans who, post mortem, existed in some other state, maybe in caves in the Himalayas, and continued to teach advanced esoterics.

> *'UFO expert Tim Good said: "It is quite conceivable beings from outer space would be aware of what Windsor Castle is and who stays there."'*
>
> *- Sunday Mirror, March 9th 1986*

In a sense, the study of Aeonics is the appreciation of the symbols which recur in popular vision. People from our technological culture, steeped in the mythos of science, are aware that it is quite likely that other planets have achieved space travel, just as the Mediaeval mind, steeped in christianity, would not consider visits from angels as unlikely. But what are the UFO visions trying to tell us?

UFO sightings seem to have begun in the 1940s, and may have peaked in the '70s, at least at the major sites such as Warminster. Despite the above report, the sightings may well have tailed off. What is more interesting in the present context is how occultists have dealt with the phenomenon.

The concept of extraterrestrial intelligences predates the sightings somewhat, as mentioned in the last section. Crowley began at some stage to consider Aiwass as 'extraterrestrial'. Dion Fortune promoted the identification of Da'ath with Sirius and 'transdimensional' or extraterrestrial 'contacts'. Kenneth Grant's *Typhonian OTO* has extended these concepts to create a 'Nightside' to the Tree of Life, reached through Da'ath and relating to ET intelligences.

A direction begins to emerge: the Tree of Life is a planar system, relating to the conscious mind or *tonal,* and reflecting the convergence of mundane (in the original sense) thought processes. Through leaving the conscious mind, entering the *nagual,* one merges with the (seemingly) irrational processes of the organic world; linear structures give way to the coiling, branching patterns of the atavistic non-self. This was driven into the cultural unconscious by the patriarchal religions, and so is identified with the nightside, the Tunnels of Set, and, of course, the Goddess. In dissolving the cultural ego, one is reaching out to the source of true intelligence, whose patterns are as yet unmanifest. These patterns are symbolized by the ET intelligences, streaming through the local star-gate at Sirius. Since they relate to the future, these intelligences are also related to time-travel. The title of the Aeonic communication received by Soror Andahadna of the Ma'at Cabal is *The Book of the Foreshadowing of the Feather,* suggesting that the book is to be read as a foreshadowing of a future *Aeon of Ma'at,* of Truth and Justice, which is (by the wonderful paradoxes of time-travel) already coexistent with the warlike Aeon of Horus. This coexistence is seen as occurring in the minds of those magicians who have identified with the creation of this Aeon.

To return to the question, the UFO phenomenon may be seen as a reaching out towards a new and better Aeon. Since space travel, we have been able to see the planet from the outside instead of just the surface. According to Goedel's Theorem, no system can view itself in its totality; it has to jump up a level to the metasystem which includes it. We need to view the planet as a whole if we are to survive this cusp age.

CHANGING MECHANISMS: POLITICAL DEMONOLOGY

History does not flow forward smoothly, with human minds responding easily to new energies and manifesting them in their lives. Those who are manifesting new awareness find themselves working against the inertia of the old. Everything that exists had, at one time, life, and maybe purpose. Many institutions and social codes evolved out of a now-vanished new awareness and manifested a new facet of the human race mind, a new Aeon, in their time. As often as not, they had already lost their inner impulse and become decadent by the time they had reached the stage of codes and institutions. It is the nature of consolidation, like good intentions, to pave the road to hell, and there is no stench like the odour of sanctity when it has passed its shelf-life.

Fortunately for the individual, institutions are incapable of much intelligence, operating as they do on the lowest-common-denominator principle. The modern magician, when faced with social opposition, tends to work in secret, to outwit the lumbering dinosaurs of official society. However, if this simple kind of stupidity was all that was opposed to him, he would be able to rise in any direction he chose, simply by the advantage that living a double life gives one. But awesome, grinding, inertial force seems to keep people of sound mind and good will from exercising much influence. Why? A Marxist, in answer, might refer to our outmoded economic systems, a Christian to Original Sin. It is unlikely that a magician would be entirely satisfied with either answer. Rather, it is more a case of looking for a paradigm than looking for answers.

One formulation, by no means complete, is the Mind Parasite paradigm. This is to be found almost exclusively in the guise of fiction, and is aptly expressed by the following passage:

> *'Kim now realises that they can take over our bodies and minds and use them for their own purposes. So why do they always take over stupid, bigoted people, or people who are retarded or psychotic? Obviously they are looking for dupes and slaves, not for intelligent allies. In fact their precise intention is to destroy human intelligence, to blunt human awareness and to block human beings out of space. What they are launching is an extermination program. And anyone who has sufficient insight to suspect the existence of a they is a prime target'*
> *- Wiliam S. Burroughs, The Place of Dead Roads*

These transcorporeal criminals turn up in stories under the guises of macrobes, Nova Mob, mind parasites, 'clever devils'. They are the core topic of a whole new literary demonology, spilling over into conspiracy theories, appearing as unobserved controllers of the 'heads' of the 'body politic', desperately paranoid models to explain the bizarre twists and paradoxes of global viciousness and stupidity. The mechanisms of late-patriarchal politics are ideally suited to their program: occupying whole populations in a latent state, they appear in an active state in the politicians who reflect these populations, who in turn feed them back, via the media, to the public, whose fears are thereby reinforced. The process is analogous to the life cycle of a virus or other obligate parasite, the two stages being population and politician, and the transfer vector being the media.

So what hope is there? Following the virus analogy, first one removes oneself from the infection cycle. Magicians are already doing this, by retraining their minds not to respond to the dominant nonsense, but to respond instead to the inner drives, insights and intuitions. Tremendous strength is required to sustain this drive in the face of the received stupidities. Cooperation is required, and is made awesomely difficult because of the native individualism of magicians, or because of residual imprints of society's power relations. The cusp age or Chaos groups are conspiracies of liberation, generating magical singularities where the laws of the consensus reality do not apply. This is the most secret level of a process which is multi-levelled; each individual is a centre whose circumference is nowhere to be found, and each group is a prototype Web of living energy, manifesting its resistance to the virus through the liberation of its members as well as its visible actions. Victory, which is to say survival, is not assured; the work must be its own reward, or it won't work.

From Issue 3: The Slope of Words Collage: The head be unreeled

William Burroughs had a strange sideways influence on me as my magical world was developing. I first read *Naked Lunch* at age 18 and was gripped by some of the scenes and ideas in it, but I can't honestly say I understood the point of all of it. But as I read more of Burroughs's fiction in my 20s, I started to grasp that it was all one thing, one vast sprawling book, some sections of which were unreadable, some astonishingly elegant, some very entertaining and amusing. One big book about power, oppression and how it's programmed into us, and a quest for a magic that helps liberate us when all other approaches have failed. Together with Phil Hine I co-wrote a piece about the magic in Burroughs's books called 'Operation Overload'. It appeared in *CI5* but since this was more Phil's work than mine, I don't include it here.

I experimented with cut-up and collage as magical techniques, and wrote a couple of pieces, one included here in a later section. I also made some graphics from collaged words; *The head be unreeled* is an example. This led on to making textual patterns in runic spell-collages, see the *Tiwaz* and *Kenaz* spells at the end of Part 3.

The head be unreeled was built from a series of poetic fragments which I was frustrated with. They included reflections on landscape magic and the end of a relationship. Cut up was a way of losing the narrative I was trying to impose, which was tainted with unhappiness, and forefronting the moments of value in a fresh new way.

I typed the poems out, cut them into their lines and shuffled those around. Then I pasted them round in a circle, using Pritt stick, leaving a central void. I liked the resulting pattern, but knew it needed more work. What to do with that void in the middle?

In those days, people did cutups with craft knives and glue, then often created new effects using a photocopier. You'd take your embryonic cutup pages to some business or institution and pay them a few pence per A4 sheet to run them through their office's black and white Xerox machines.[11] I used some reduction to get a circle of text that was a bit smaller. Hmm, interesting. But it's still got a hole in the middle. I kept reducing the collage size with

[11] The 'A' paper sizes are a beautiful idea: the aspect ratio is the Golden Mean ratio, approximately 1.618:1. The ratio is conserved when you fold the paper in half. It makes Foolscap and other aspect ratios look rather foolish.

successive photocopies until the text was illegible, a dark obscurity in the centre, a decorative plunge into incoherence. Finally, I took all the various reductions, cut out the circles of text with their central holes cut out and pasted them over one another. Yes! I'd got what I wanted—the text was transformed, the magic was achieved.

The resulting collage was, as you can see, made of five or six layers of 70 or 80gsm paper, plus the black card base. It had become a 3D thing.

THE SLOPE OF WORDS

The intercutting of obsessional material generated by automatic writing is a powerful tool for exploring the nightside and developing a personal twilight language. Imagine language as a spectrum, running from conscious articulation, rational meaning, through sleep-talk and irrational meanings, babbling or glossolalia ('monstrous' speech), to the primal screaming and howling of infantile or atavistic resurgence. Just as our biological history is recapitulated through the resurgence of DNA atavisms, so does speech contain layers of verbal history, residues of Aeonic time-zones extending back to pre-verbal strata of personal and racial 'memory'. The most primal strata of language lie at the Hermetic core of magick, of words as cosmos-creating.

An example of the use of this principle is seen in the Angelic languages of John Dee and Edward Kelly; the first angelic language uttered by Kelly seems more or less glossolalia, consisting of a repetitious babble with no grammatical structure. The later language of the Enochian Calls comes with an English translation, has rudimentary grammar, and echoes surviving languages: English, Latin, Greek, Hebrew etc. It is as if Kelly's fertile imagination had cut up the scholarly magickal languages of the time, half-remembered word-strings culled from Dee's library, or by telepathic access to Dee's vast scriptural knowledge. The result is a language imitative of conscious speech but soaked through with the power and mystique of the liminal twilight, suggestive of incredible gulfs of time. It is interesting to note that the first new Angelic names were generated almost literally by cut-up: writing Hebrew planetary Names diagonally into a square and then reading across.

'No-one can conceal what is saying cut-up... You can cut the Truth out of any written or spoken words' as Burroughs claims; it is as if Dee and Kelly had cut up the scriptures in an attempt to arrive at 'true knowledge'. Enochian is just one example. A more recent one might be Lovecraft, whose Old Ones sound vaguely like Egyptian gods, an idea developed by Kenneth Grant, who in turn uses the twisting tracks of gematria to draw the reader into the twilight of speech.

The development of twilight language may begin with residues of former negative feelings and frustrations. During phases of aridity, the automatisms that arise have the feel of dead ends to them, as if the magician, having taken a particular turn in life, suddenly finds that it has led to a condition of paralysing ennui. This kind of automatism is a premature ending to a false start—one's life-direction has curled away from true and is exhausting itself in a spasm of self-negation. Like a giant star, if it had sufficient mass—which is to say significance—it may collapse completely, taking the incautious observer with it into functional depression.

Near the inner horizon of this event, the mind detects strange half-formed concepts, the intimate data of nightmare, belonging to the past and yet containing the codes for future transformation. Poisoned by negative association, they cannot be decoded directly, but form the raw material for a special kind of cut-up procedure.

Arbitrary rearrangement of these alien residues detaches them from their original habit patterns and introduces links which expand the tiny vortices of locked-in force, dismantling dysfunctional desire-configurations and enabling them to recrystallise into a new direction. This generation of motion out of a closed cycle is analogous to bringing a demon under will through discovery of its twilight name. Success in this type of operation lays the ground for easier successes in the future, and is likely to lead to the discovery of unsuspected energies and creative powers.

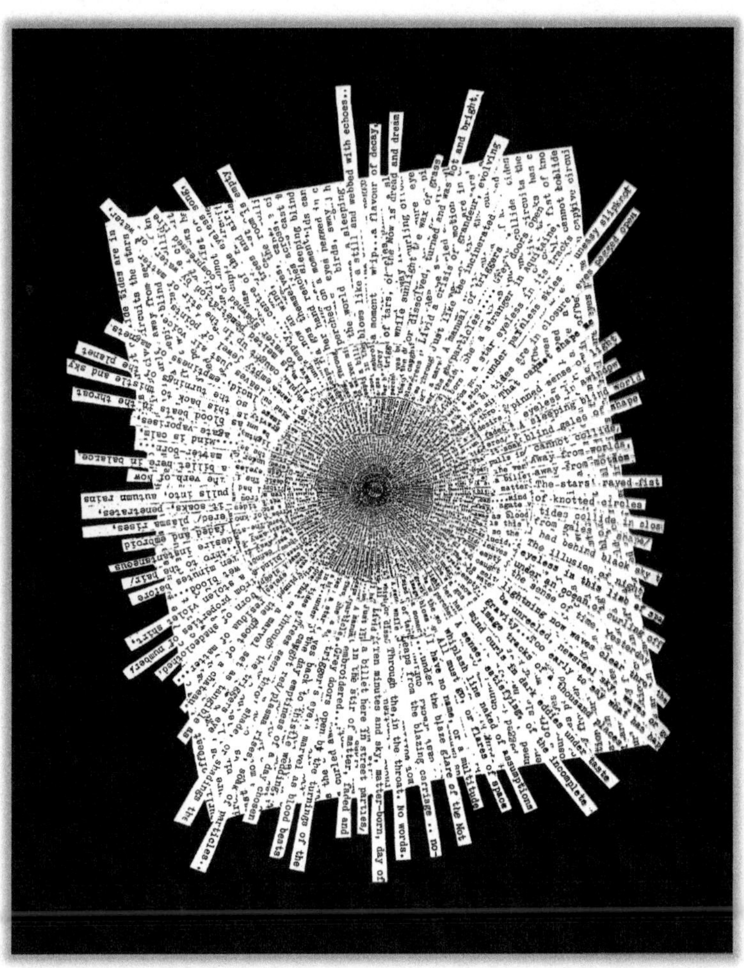

Capimao Vovim (Timedragon): an invocation of serpent time

Timesnake was part of a lengthy semi-automatic text I wrote in 1987 under the influence of LSD. It appeared in *Chaos International* no.3. Subsequently, first-wave chaos magician Charles Brewster announced an Enochian Poetry competition, and I thought it would be just the thing for that, so I translated it as closely as I could. The Enochian language has a small vocabulary that's highly specialized in areas of mystic ecstasy and cosmic terror; you can say *hyacinth pillars of eternity* but not *where is the shop?* So the English words of the original are lost in translation, but replaced by something with quite a different flavour. I reproduce both versions below, with the Enochian retranslated to English.

This poem was recorded with music on the *Timedragons* album, which is available from Falcon Press.

TIMESNAKE

Glimpsed as Time unfolds Her lazy belly
Scales flash,
        in Her coils of mortal fear
The words
        that are a glint of light on dust
Hammered bright,
        then dark and burdened
                with the weight of all their years
Immortal and ceaseless, swallowed by Her eyes,
Grown forth as new
And, although your self cannot be separate from Hers,
She is the greater, and he the lesser
in whose lesser eye the vaster coils are seen
Approach and slither
into their beaten words
and in whose drama Her coils are reared,
She is named for stars, cascades of Her coils
chased by a god's giant eye
And in a shock awakens to himself
        as though a wisp of dream
                or flake of moss
                        clung to his once-buried lips
Where, kissed by other kings, Her soil and roots
Had sought him out
Aeons, breathless and blind
Her coils a cage for his heart
Until
Robed and stroked by Her breath
Glazing the long coils of blood
Until
        spiralling up again in a shout, and tentative
His voice is heard, unchoked by dough, leaf-mould
        dark and wily resistance
A child weaned, at once to yell, in his concentrated quickness
out of the spring, the uncoiled coil of Her laughter -
- *See? It wasn't so hard!*
And as long as I give thee breath
What is there to fear?

CAPIMAO VOVIM

URANAH CA CAPIMAO ODONAH TILBEH IPSORIS UNALABEH

seen as time opens her lazy skirts

OLPIRTEH LORSELQUE A TILBEH COMSELHEH DE TELOACH HOXMARCHEN

lights flower in her circles of deadly fear,

A LOGAAH AR I A CACAOM DE OLPIRTEH CEH PAPNOREA

the speech that is the flourish of light on memories

FARZEMEH DE LUCIFTIAS OD OLNE ORELA OD AMMAHA

raised to brilliance, and made dark and cursed

AA CAPIMIALI DE COCASBEH

with eternity of time

GOHED IALPONEH A TILBEH OOANOAN UGEGI CAPIMALI

everlasting, burned by her eyes, grown strong time after time

OD G MANIN I GE TELIOBEH DE TILBEHE,

and your mind is not separate from hers,

PI I DRILPI OD TIA A IPTIA, I CASARMAN IPTIA OOAONA

she is the greater, and he the lesser, in whose lesser eye

A DRILPI COMSELHEH CHIIS URANAH, NIISA OD YOLCAM

the greater circles are seen, come and bring forth

PAR IALPOR LOGAAH

their burning speech

OD I CASARMAN OSFEH TILBEH COMSELHEH CHIIS GOHOLOREH

and in whose discord her circles are raised,

PI I DOOAINEH DE AOIVEAE, A PANPIRAE DE TILBEH COMSELHEH

she is named for stars, the cascades of her circles,

FAFEH DE DRILPA OOAONA DE MADEH

followed by the great eye of a god

OD DO MOLVI TORZURPE DE TOX NOMIG VEP DE DOSIG

and in a surge awakens to himself, even as a flame of night

GEH LONCHOAH LORSELQEH AMIZPIEH DE TIA GOHEDA TELOCHEH ADOIAN

or falling flower fastened to his once dead face

QUIIN BLANSARA TELOCHE MADAN, BABALOND DORPHALDEH TIA

where, sheltering dead gods, the harlot sought him
HOMINEH TELOCHE DE GIGIPAH OD URANNAH
ages, dead of breath and sight,
TILBEH COMSELHEH OOGE DE TIA MONONSEH CACERAG
her circles a chamber for his heart, until
ZONAC OD OBLOCEH DE TILBEH GIGIPAH, ALDI A DRILPA
clothed and garlanded by her breath gathering the great
COMSELHEH DE CNILA, CACERAGE TORZULPEH I DRILPA BAHAL
circles of blood, until, arising in a great cry
AMGEDE PHAE
begun anew,
TIA CAMLIAXEH I TOATARAH GEALLAR DE FABOAN DE UNCHIAH
his speech is heard unbound from poison, from confounders,
UGEGIAH, BAHAL DE TIA MICALZO, DE TIA IAODEH
waxing strong, to cry out in his power, out of his beginning,
A GECOMSEHELEDEN COMSELHEH DE TILBEH MOZEH
the uncircled circle of her joy
URAN! DA IPAM EOPHAN, OD CAPIMAO DLUGAM NONCA UGEAR,
see! it is not sorrow! and as long as I give you strength,
DARSAR I DA HOXMARCH?
what is there to fear?

From Issue 12: Seven Small Sorceries of Smell
Co-written with Claire Fennell

Since childhood, I've been enchanted by smells. We had honeysuckle in the garden when I was small, and its aroma framed July for me, just as the smell of fireworks made November what it was. Then later, acid opened me up to that hyper-intense smell thing, where a waft of incense can send you reeling into a new ecstasy. At Glastonbury Fayre in 1971, I smelled real, resin-based incense; the only previous time had been an otherwise-unremarkable childhood visit to some High Anglican Church. So the encounter with that festival stall at Glasto was really the first time, and I felt that I'd discovered something which had been missing all my life.

When I got into magical practice, I dove into studying aromatics with the intention of mastering their use. By 1979 I was starting to make incenses for myself, then for friends who asked for them. For my starting-point attributions I used Crowley's *Liber 777*. However, there simply aren't enough resin and oil attributions in that list to make most of the planetary incenses. I needed more. I got Paul Huson's *Mastering Herbalism*, which had a chapter on making incenses; that was literally all there was in print on the subject at that time. I tried out a few of his recommendations and experimented. I would go to the Sorcerer's Apprentice every couple of weeks and buy a different herb or resin and try smouldering it on hot charcoal. If I liked it, or at least found it interesting, I'd find out more about its properties and attributions.

After a year or so of this, I had my own sets of attributions to work with. Eventually I wrote my first book, *Magical Incense*,[12] the book I wished I'd been able to read when I first started out.

---

[12] Lee D. (1991). *Magical Incenses*, Revelations 23 Press.

SEVEN SMALL SORCERIES OF SMELL

Most magicians are aware that the sense of smell is widely underrated and are familiar with the use of incenses to provide atmospheres and mnemonic keys to magically useful states of mind. The following article is less a set of formulated recipes than a range of suggestions intended to generate some fresh ideas for the use of aromatics in magic.

Modern research into the physiology and biochemistry of plant extracts confirms some of the predictions of the pre-scientific psychology of magical correspondences. Working from both directions—traditional and science—we can distil the information most useful to the magician.

Workings for Self-Confidence, Personal Power, Psychic wholeness for self and others are enhanced by Frankincense. The resin granules collected from the dried sap of *Boswellia thurifera*, Olibanum or Frankincense have been prized as incense for millennia. Of the twin attributions to Sun and Moon, the Solar aspect is supported by the action of frankincense on human metabolism. The distilled oil generates a deep feeling of warmth, and deepens breathing, assisting positive emotional states. Its aroma is often described as 'glorious'.

Suggestions: use two drops of the oil in a ritual or pre-ritual bath or anointing oil. Burn the resin as incense.

Spells for love, sex and pleasure naturally suggest Rose. Rose oil acts as an antidepressant, aphrodisiac and uterine tonic, confirming its age-old association with the female sexual organs. Jasmine oil, traditionally attributed to the Moon, shares the antidepressant and aphrodisiac properties of rose, and acts as a stimulant to the central nervous system. According to the work of Professor Dodds of Warwick University, jasmine oil is more stimulating gram for gram than caffeine. The aroma of jasmine has the heady voluptuousness one would expect, with an underlying note reminiscent of the 'rude' animal quality of civet: this is due to indole, a substance that forms the molecular framework of one group of psychoactive drugs. The combination of jasmine and rose must be the most successful match in the best commercial perfumes of traditional type—pure Venusian sorcery!

Suggestions: Jasmine, Rose or both in anointing oils. They are both rather expensive to use on an oil evaporator for most purposes, but tiny amounts go a very long way in blends. Use rose petals in incenses and pot-pourris for perfuming a place of working. Synthetic rose and jasmine oils have no physiological action, but can be included in incenses for their psychological effects.

For the projection of healing energies, material bases involving oils of Lavender or Chamomile are invaluable. Lavender is the most useful of therapeutic oils, with a vast and well-studied range of actions on tissues: it is anti-inflammatory, antiseptic, and stimulates cellular reproduction, amongst other virtues. It appears to be adaptogenic, normalizing physiological processes, and its psychological effects are calming and equilibrating. German Chamomile, from *Matricaria camomilla* is a deep-blue oil, the blue being due to azulene, an intensely anti-inflammatory substance.

Suggestions: the qualities of Lavender and Blue Chamomile (and, to a lesser extent, Roman and Moroccan type chamomiles) make it easy to visualize an intense, soft-blue radiance to carry intentions of the 'Heal Thyself' type. This is obviously greatly potentiated if the recipient actually has some of the same oil.

Aggressive magics are traditionally associated with such substances as Red Peppers. The volatile oils of peppers increase blood flow, acting as stimulants, and generating the 'red face' of the Martial gnosis.

Suggestions: burn incenses involving Mustard Seeds, both for their stimulating, pungent smoke and for the explosive pops. Evaporating oil of Black Pepper provides a subtler kind of Martial sensation.

Learning and thinking magics are assisted by the stimulant oils Rosemary and Basil. The borneol camphors of rosemary act powerfully on the nervous system—in fact rosemary oil should not be used if you suffer from epilepsy or high blood pressure. The effect is enhanced by mixing in some basil oil. In some traditions, rosemary herb was used for banishing—its fresh aroma and the increased alertness it gives make it ideal.

Suggestions: for mental magics, mental acrobatics or prolonged concentration, try evaporating a mixture of mostly rosemary oil with a little basil.

Hypnosis, twilight states may be enhanced by oil of Marjoram. This essential oil is profoundly sedative, acting to lower blood pressure and sex drive.

Suggestion: try evaporating marjoram oil as a background to threshold-of-sleep workings.

'Pure' or 'Octarine' Magic: there are a small group of odours which generate quite different associations to any of the above categories. In particular, the resinoid Galbanum has an odd, fantastic quality; it often gives a sense of space, or mysterious darkness, with hints of the synthetic aromas of plastics. Related aromas are Oakmoss resinoid and Labdanum.

Suggestions: for Uranian/Octarine workings, try compounding an incense of Galbanum, Mastic (or Dammar), Oakmoss, Opopanax and Dittany of Crete.

Magical Views of Consciousness

One of my longer CI pieces, the two-parter 'Beyond the Soft Machine' found its way into my book *Chaotopia!*,[13] so I'm not including it here. It dealt with a quantum-physics-based physical theory—the Bose-Einstein Condensate model of consciousness—for how magic might work. This idea has not lasted well—the putative basis for the condensed state in neural tissue, the Fröhlich ion pump, has been shown to be classical rather than quantum in action. But at the time I found the theory very exciting—a candidate for the missing step in the mechanism of how mind influences the world. Even Peter Carroll's physicalist theory of magic lacks this element.

But that missing-step problem is of a piece with the so-called 'hard problem' of consciousness in philosophy, insofar as it is an artefact that arises from the rigid Cartesian dualism of mind and matter. From the point of view of panpsychism, the problem dissolves away—it's no surprise that we are conscious, because consciousness rests on fundamental properties of physical particles. From an Idealist point of view (see for instance Bernardo Kastrup) there's no problem either; what we call consciousness and matter are different phases or aspects of mind.

I got less interested in coding magic or consciousness as physics. But the other obsession, to view mystical states and practices without the dogmatism, didn't go away. I was determined to apply the same experimental anti-dogmatic approach to mystical practice and results that succeeded in practical magic. I made tentative steps in that direction with my 1997 book *Chaotopia!*, my first full-length book on magic-in-general. The book was a *hypersigil*,[14] a spell in itself, with the intention of bringing about a chaos-magic like current of investigation into higher consciousness and mystical practice.

I would say it succeeded—not long after *Chaotopia!*'s first edition, Julian Vayne and Greg Humphries brought out *Now That's What I Call Chaos Magic*, which had a considerable section on Holy Guardian Angel work and experiences, and then a few years after that Alan Chapman, someone who'd come into the magical scene through chaos magic, produced his *Advanced Magic For Beginners*, and began to launch himself as a spiritual teacher.

---

[13] Lee D. (2006). *Chaotopia!*, Mandrake of Oxford.

[14] 'Hypersigil' is a term coined by writer Grant Morrison to describe some of his books, which worked not only as works of art in the conventional sense but also as spells which changed the writer's life.

From Issue 16:
Buddy, Can You Spare a Paradigm?

I gave a talk at the second UKAOS public meeting in London's Conway Hall on Wealth Magic. Having a decent or even reasonably regular income was one of the final larger bits of practical magic to fall into place for me. Since I'd stopped being a research scientist at Leeds University I'd gone through a number of jobs, spanning from agricultural labourer via bar manager to library assistant. But I hadn't found an entirely satisfactory solution to the problem of getting a steady income without the soul-destroying horror of having a mainstream job.

I started doing all kinds of wealth and money magics, and talking and writing about the ones that worked. One of the first things I learned to articulate is the difference between money and wealth. I go into that in this article. For more, see *The Wealth Magic Workbook*.[15]

Have my attitudes towards wealth and money changed since then? Not substantially, though the old adage about doing your true will and being assisted by the momentum of the universe has eventually proven much truer than I used to give it credit for.

[15] Lee D. (1994). *The Wealth Magic Workbook*, Attractor Press.

BUDDY, CAN YOU SPARE A PARADIGM? MONEY AND WEALTH

This article is about doing magic for wealth and money. To begin with, I shall define my terms: what is Money, and what is Wealth?

Money does not constitute wealth. Naturally, if you are wealthy, you have sufficient money at any moment. Similarly, if you have a 'large' sum of money, you can live a wealthy life if you want to. But the terms Money and Wealth are not interchangeable: the person who inherits or wins half a million could, with an enjoyable degree of effort, ensure a ready supply of money for the rest of any lifespan. Or blow it in no time at all.

In the words of the song, money won't change you. But wealth will; wealth is an attitude.

This is where the significant difference between wealth magic and other magics comes in. You are unlikely to succeed if you just do a sigil for wealth. A servitor-elemental, permanently functioning in the etheric dimensions, is nearer the mark. We are looking at a long-term change here. The basic skills of Enchantment and Evocation may not, on their own, be enough. We need to work in the disciplines of Invocation and Illumination, to converse with Gods and to reprogram our expectations, to find, if you like, a metaprogrammer state from which to renegotiate the conditions of the selves. To put it simply, money is to wealth like sex drive is to skill at sexual relationships.

Money is a parameter, whose value is arbitrary and impersonal; Wealth is a skill, whose value is arbitrary, and personal. Money is a Spirit, an elemental; Wealth is the attribute of a God.

Let us look at the attributes of this Spirit of Money. The Money Spirit can be seen as mindless or nearly mindless. This gives rise to the popular image of Mammon, a force of blind and brutal greed. However, this image is judgmental, and too imprecise for our purposes. I think of the Money Spirit as being like the great Elemental Kings of the Enochian psychocosm, with their endless Names of howling and soughing vowels. A vast, impersonal elemental force, money flows and flashes down the circuits of communication systems, its true Name hidden in its countless billions upon billions of alphanumeric digits.

The Nature of Money is reproduction, movement. It withers if kept still; it loves to move. It's enormously powerful. People love it and hate it in a variety of ways.

These restless Mercurial qualities of the money spirit, its affinity with communication hierarchies and networks, has led to a suggestion that Air would be a better elemental attribution than Discs of Earth. There is some usefulness in this idea—if we can get away from the idea of money as coins in our pockets, we are one step closer to the concept of Wealth.

Our relationship to money changes in a way that can be described by the three Gunas, or the Alchemical Triad of Sulphur, Mercury and Salt. In the tarot trump called The Wheel, the three principles in the guise of atavisms rotate endlessly. The magic medium of money shifts through three phases. In terms of conventional economics, the phases might be Growth, Inflation and Recession. I'll leave the details of that to the more economically minded, but the mechanisms are profoundly chaotic, like the mechanisms of the weather. For the individual, these phases might be represented by: Getting an Income, Shopping and Being Skint. The Wheel of Fortune turns, and your fortunes change with each movement.

Let us move on and look at the nature of Wealth, the kind of consciousness that forms successful relationships with the Money Spirit. What is wealth? I would define it as confidence, competence and abundant pleasure in your material conditions. Living your life as you wish. The magic of wealth entails identifying the sphere of material power and competence you desire and phenomenizing it.

THE HIERARCHY OF FREEDOM

The distinction between wealth and money can be spread over a spectrum, illustrating the different emphases that magic will have at each level:

* The wealthy individual is free, enjoying the material resources he desires, playing with the kingly grace of a creature at the top of a food chain, a big cat or bird of prey. The world of a truly wealthy person is held together by a resource of joyous power that stems from the experience of radical freedom at the innermost core, the quantum chaos of consciousness. Without the will to play confidently in the world, everything stays at the crudest and most temporary level of money magic.
* The next level down, the magician realizes that the only things worth enchanting for are experiences, conditions of life which fulfil his dreams. The identification of one's driving dream, and the knowledge of the resources needed to realise it, form a large part of the work at this level.
* The spectrum now slides away from freedom, towards enslavement, towards obsessional insecurity about money. Many people who are competent at making money are terribly insecure about their survival and status, so that their money does not bring them wealth in the above sense—only more obsession with making more money, which is hardly freedom. Such people are workaholics or wage slaves. Each day, each pay-cheque, each repetition of the same meaningless task—this is the key to the demonic aspect of the money spirit, that its mastery over you will lead to immersion in boring repetition and routine.

* The worst condition is the *poverty well*. Like a gravity well, this warps perspective. It pulls wealth and money together so that they can't be disentangled. In the poverty well, the only parameter is cash. The poor person is enslaved to money, and will often do anything to get it. In this state, money is all-important, a continual emergency, much of the content of one's internal dialogue.

The following sections take the themes of Wealth magick and money magick separately and suggest some approaches.

WEALTH MAGIC ILLUMINATION AND INVOCATION

When working for wealth, the object of Illumination is Wealth Consciousness, the organic belief in the existence and inevitability of wealth for you.

This aspect of Wealth Magic is summed up in the symbol of the Sphere of Availability. I came across this concept in a book by Ophiel with the wonderfully evocative title of *How to Get Material Things by Creative Visualization*. Ophiel tells the story of a man who was so poor that he lived in one room without even a carpet. After many days staring at his floor, he began to visualize a little rug there. The next day, he goes out and finds a nice scrap of carpet, perhaps in a skip. He goes on to visualize his world bit by bit, building it up until he becomes a very wealthy man.

The moral of the tale is that he could not have done all this in one step—that when he was poor, his Zone of Availability was down to a single item. When he had acquired that, he was able to visualize other, more expensive possessions, so that only by successive acquisitions did his ability to visualize his wealth grow. Get yourself used to being wealthy, thinking wealthy. Build on each success, always expanding. The formula here is *BIGGER*:

Banish negativity

Invoke with

Grand

Gestures

Enchant and Evoke

Reorganize and Prepare

The Royal Road of Illumination in wealth magic seems to me to be Invocation. Consider the Gods and Goddesses of Wealth and Fortune—Jupiter, Ganesha, Zeus, Hera, Mamiwater: they are mature, serene, jovial, powerful, charismatic, confident, optimistic, positive. Work with the Gods and Goddesses of Wealth and Fortune in invocation, so that you summon their aid, and become more like them yourself. Salute the expansive greatness, the massive confidence of these beings. Surround yourself with symbols of your God or Goddess, with symbols of wealth and generosity. Exalt your feelings in love and admiration to these beings, until you begin to identify with their awesome power.

MONEY MAGICKS – ENCHANTMENT AND EVOCATION

In money evocation we are forming a relationship with the spirit of money and bringing some part of that spirit-power under our control. As a first step to this, pay more attention to money.

* When someone hands you money, look at the coins, the notes, the cheques. Banknotes in particular are complex talismans, beautiful and somewhat mysterious. Acquaint yourself with these magic pictures.
* Meditate on the universality of money, the way it turns up everywhere.
* Consider the uniformity of notes and coins.
* Consider money as biosurvival tokens.
* Reflect on the meaning to the other of parting with money, and the meaning to you of receiving it.
* Consider the things the Money Spirit likes and dislikes.
* Make it your friend.
* Love it.

For a virtual experience of the money spirit, and the construction of a servitor from it, try ***the following pathworking***.

> *What is the first image of money that comes to mind? Hold it as a visual image steady in your gaze. It is a doorway, which swings open in a storm of glittering dust.*
>
> *You step out onto a grey space, the air like packed dust pressing against your senses. Then you detect a humming, a throb which appears to be in the bass section but moves through the whole spectrum to ultrasound.*
>
> *Suddenly, the grey shatters and you are moving at speed through a flat, synthetic landscape with intermittent organic forms. You are moving so fast you cannot identify these. The cyberscape is a blur of colour, with a sparking blue haze.*
>
> *Rise up through the matrix, up, up through the swarming information streams. You rise until you are floating high above the details of the cyberscape. You are in a part of the matrix that is flooded with sparkling light which tingles through you with exquisite pleasure. You look up, through the seething brilliance, to where a gigantic Chaosphere hangs.*
>
> *Know this: From the source of pure chaos comes the brilliance of mind, wherein is the true home of the Spirit of Money. As you gaze into the space*

before you, something takes shape. A macroform condenses out of the ubiquitous light, egg shaped at first, and then taking on the outlines of your entity. It trembles in the light, held in place by the tension of your gaze.

Now reach into the centre, touching the substance of the servitor, and instruct it as you will.

A final point about money magick. Organize your life so that you are always creating new inlets for money. When you work for large sums of money, make sure you have opened plenty of channels for manifestation. Otherwise you may get it by your Uncle Ernest dropping dead and leaving you your stake in his will, or your lover being crippled in an accident and getting compensation.

THE ECONOMIC, IMPERSONAL SYSTEM

There is a curious phrase which is commonplace in media economics: 'confidence'. This appears to mean trading expectations, as polled from various businesspeople and pundits. Stagnant economies can be re-inflated by a burst of 'confidence'. What we have here is a self-fulfilling prophecy, and anywhere we find self-fulfilling prophecies, we are in a magic-sensitive environment. The adventurous magical businessperson might like to take this idea and, using the concept of 'confidence' as a magical emotion, attempt to influence the macro system.

Fade out to the monkeybabble of a dealing floor in a boom phase...

From Issue 17: The Cyberzoo

As chaos magicians how do we work with spirits? In the early chaos magic books that area of magic was under-emphasized, because the spirit model of magical action is much more challenging to Scientism than are the others.

To unpack that idea a bit, I'll use Ralph Tegtmeier's idea of five models of magic or, as he called them, paradigms.[16]

The *Psychological Paradigm* models magic as pretty much 'all in the mind'. How our magical actions shape our world doesn't come as a built-in part of this paradigm. Furthermore, what the mind consists of and how much of it is inside our skulls is an issue which makes this paradigm rather leaky—it tends to approach or even overlap other paradigms. For instance, if we take the view that our awareness consists of the interplay between elements in a network, we are close to the following magical model, Information.

The *Information Paradigm* may be the newest, or the oldest, from some standpoints. This model sits nicely with an awareness of how our identities emerge in a web of interactions with other conscious beings, as well as the current fad for the idea that we live in a simulation.

In a full-blown *Energy paradigm*, magic is considered to happen by means of 'energies' travelling from one place to another.

The *Spirit Paradigm* is one in which our magic is done by independent, deceased, or non-human agencies with which we negotiate. A strong example of a full-time spirit paradigm approach would be that of a Voudon or Santeria practitioner.

The limitations of all the above 'paradigms' is what makes it important for the magician to avail themselves of all four models, switching to one model to utilize its strengths before shifting to another to avoid its weaknesses, and utilize the strengths of a different way of seeing the world. This is what the fifth paradigm, the *Meta Model*, consists of.

For a flavour of the Meta-Model, imagine how a helper spirit, or what a chaos magician might term a 'servitor', would appear in each:

- To a full-time Spirit magician, everything has a spirit, and you talk and negotiate with them. The servitor is another entity in a world teeming with various kinds of sentience.
- To someone who takes the Psychological model as foremost, a servitor is basically a set of instructions inhabiting your nervous system, very similar to the idea of a Strategy in NLP.

---

[16] Can be found online as: MODELS OF MAGIC, by Frater U.'.D.'.

* To the Energy magician, a servitor is a self-sustaining net of energy with an inbuilt purpose.
* To our Cybermagician, the servitor is a net of information among other nets of information.
* To be able to switch between these viewpoints at will is the essence of Chaos Magic.

I tried to make the four viewpoints sound as if they had equal weight, but it's obvious that the closest model to our dominant culture's Scientism is the Psychological. The Information paradigm is almost respectable, and the Energy model is not so far off but the Spirit model really grinds Scientism's dogma gears.

The fact that spirit magic had more or less been excluded by the physicalist bias of Pete Carroll's early work was a worthy challenge, part of a necessary stripping down of magical theory before it could be built up again, but I'm pleased to see spirit work entering into the chaos magic discourse these days.

In this article I describe magic as 'an elite preoccupation'; that strikes me now as a bit of an over-the-top swagger, but it's something I've revisited again and again over the years—the extreme rarity of people who live full-time magical lives—and I touch on it again in Part 4.

THE CYBERZOO: MAKING SENSE OF SPIRIT PARADIGMS

> *He's got so many servitors*
> *His magic never fails*
> *His dinner's always made for him*
> *By things with claws and scales*
> *- (from a sorcerers' drinking song, early 21st Century)*
> *It takes centuries to make a god. Of course, you could make one a lot quicker, but it would be a crap god.*
> *- The Ape of Thoth*

Ever considered how many varieties of entities are said to exist on the Inner Planes? A cursory glance shows us sorcerers talking about servitors and tulpas, shamans talking about power animals and clan animals, magicians talking about egregores, gods, demons and elementals. There are the Qabalists with their hierarchies of Archangels, Angels, Spirits, Planetary Intelligences; there are the Angels and Great Kings of the Enochian system and, for the Theosophically inclined, Devas, Masters and so on.

Chaos magicians are often reluctant to enter fully into a spiritist paradigm, because of the risk of literally believing in it for evermore, and thereby arresting one's development at a particular stage. I have entered and left the spiritist paradigm many times, and it is indeed seductive. Anyone who has ever worked with servitors knows how convenient and effective a magical tool they can be. Anyone who has been involved in constructing a group mind entity or egregore knows how extraordinarily powerful and ultimately dangerous this tool can become. Anyone who has resonated successfully with one of the off-the-peg spirit psychocosms such as Voudon, Hoodoo or the Mediaeval Grimoires knows the lure of the power of such a system, and the strictures the magician must apply in dealing with it.

What is the common thread? And what is the nature of the danger involved? I shall describe the basic types of spirit first, then look at the features common to them.

SERVITORS are well understood, at least in practice, by Chaos magicians. They are generally simple entities, with a single purpose, or a restricted range of purposes. Occasionally, a magician might make a reprogrammable servitor, which is called upon whenever required and given a new temporary set of instructions to carry out. This type of servitor may take the form of an animal, real or mythic. However, most servitors seem to me to be less complex than most animals, appearing to the spirit vision more like a small machine, or a microchip with a limited range of information processing capacity. Creating simple servitors is a bit like welding a logic circuit together.

ELEMENTALS: In many older books, you can read Servitor for Elemental. The more general use of the term is applied to nature spirits—the spirits of earth, air, fire and water. In Golden Dawn Qabalah they are 'hunted' on the astral plane, tested by Qabalistic formulae, and then hauled back (if you're lucky and you get a good one) for use in the privacy of one's own temple. The excuse for this is that elementals like to associate with humans, because this association gives them a chance to evolve, a kind of unequal partnership deal. This is an important point which I'll come back to.

EGREGORES are group mind entities. This is quite a loose term, which is sometimes used to denote any group mind considered in the abstract, but is more meaningful when applied to a well-defined magical entity deliberately created by a group of magicians.

It also covers:

GODDESSES AND GODS can be viewed as egregores built up over centuries of adoration, terror, sexual sacrifice, blood and other familiar gnostic techniques. They tend to evolve from the totems, clan animals or hero-figures of tribes.

TOTEMS OR CLAN ANIMALS of tribes. When tribes fuse through war, one totem animal consumes another. When nations are built from tribes, the various totem animals become God/desses, as happened in the Nomes of the Egyptian civilization, the Deities of Khem arising from the different regions of the two Kingdoms.

Austin Spare reintroduced the practice of atavistic resurgence into mainstream magic. In Spare's system, an atavism is reachable by the individual magician for empowerment and sorcery, without reference to any tribe or social context. This relates the concept of animal gods to their shamanic origins, the shaman discovering his tutelary or power animal in trance, and working with it thereafter.

TULPAS: This term is Tibetan in origin. Tulpas are usually defined as thought forms, but this is a rather weak and vague description of such powerful entities. I prefer to use the term tulpa to designate a servitor or egregore entity of exceptional power, independence and programming flexibility. These entities show a distinct tendency to want to evolve, through having attention paid to them by humans. They are capable of warping reality, often spectacularly, for the magician's benefit, but the price they demand is an increase in their own intelligence and power.

William Burroughs has said 'Tulpas can get uppity', and anyone who has worked with them would surely agree.

Essentially, tulpas are personalities; Burroughs seems to be referring on one level to the experience of writing characters in his stories. It is probable that what we call personalities in ourselves have identical levels of cybernetic organization as tulpas.

Two egregore entities I have had the privilege of co-creating over the years had all of these characteristics, and I think of them as Tulpas. Eventually I chose to cease working with both of them, because they were increasingly overlapping my own field of identity. It was this set of experiences that gave rise to my speculations in this article.

Other examples of egregore entities are the GOTOS created by the *Fraternitas Saturni*, and possibly the Ascended Masters of the Golden Dawn.

DEMONS, in the sense of the Grimoires, rather than of a psychological paradigm, are quasi-intelligent, dangerous and powerful creatures with whom you have to make (and preferably keep) a pact. Their abode is Hell, which is to say an area of the inner planes ruled Out of Bounds by the monotheistic ego.

Entry to, or communication with, this realm is often done in a gnosis of fear, since it necessarily represents alienness to the dominant self. The magician separates herself radically from these entities by the use of the Circle and Triangle.

The notion of the demonic pact has at its heart the principle of employing a powerful entity in a way which satisfies the magician's feelings of having paid adequately for warping reality so greatly. To clarify this point, cast your mind back to a sigil or spell that didn't work; you can probably remember an occasion when you knew it wasn't going to work, despite the meticulous planning you had put into the working. You simply had not achieved one-pointedness: some part of your mind was not in agreement with the working and sabotaged it. As a result of such an experience, you may have evolved a technique for achieving magical unison in your selves, maybe by repeated automatic drawing on a sigil theme until it 'felt right'. Similarly, in employing a demon, the operator should enter into negotiation with it, through some system of divination or dowsing. This ensures that the final deal that is enshrined in the pact is satisfactory to both sides, that the operation is one pointed.

Similar in some ways to both demons and elementals are the *Spirits of Hoodoo* as outlined by Michael Bertiaux. These entities are also considered to be related to the souls of dead humans of great antiquity, perhaps in the sense that the ancient dead form heroic archetypes for the tribe, and eventually become identified with deities. The method of working with them magically is a form of prayer. Direct requests are made of the Spirits, and they are paid in the currency of bodily energy. The more powerful entities of this system delight in sexual sacrifice.

This is a procedure like a demonic pact, stripped down to its simplest elements, and employing less impressively alien demons.

Of course, the necessary ingredient for success is the ability to believe in the literal existence of these Spirits, to immerse oneself in the paradigm completely. This highlights one of the problems for the Chaos magician of working within off-the-peg spiritist paradigms: the spirits function only if you believe in them, and their world is highly seductive. It is seductive precisely because you are their lifeline to manifestation and evolution, and they are good at surviving and evolving. They want you—your belief, your energy, your flesh to manifest through. They don't want you to shower off your belief in them with the sweat of the last ritual.

This brings us to the central theme of this piece: that all entities seek to evolve. Evolution is development in the direction of greater complexity or, to quote Ilya Prigogine, a collapse into higher coherence. This seems to be an inherent property of all coherent information systems, or dissipative systems in Prigogine's terminology. When a clump of information can sustain its coherence by taking energy in and putting energy out, it has the kind of coherence that will take part in such an evolution. All servitors, tulpas, gods, demons, spirits and egregores must be such systems, viewed cybernetically. The tradition that elementals don't mind being ordered around by sorcerers because they want to evolve is no mere bit of superstition, but an ancient awareness of the same principle that Prigogine won the Nobel Prize for.

So where do humans fit into this scheme? I would suggest that another parameter needs to be added to make sense of our relationship to spirits. That parameter is Chaos itself.

Consider a little one-job servitor. It has few degrees of freedom; the choices that it can make are very few, and limited to finding optimum conditions for the performance of its one task.

Pretty simple. Now take a reprogrammable servitor. This is called back again and again by the wizard, resulting in its becoming more intelligent and powerful. In other words, it will, if allowed to by its master, develop more degrees of freedom, become more chaotic.

The mechanism by which a servitor or tulpa succeeds in subduing a human is simple: it is our own laziness. Laziness too is an evolutionary drive, pushing us to find ways to achieve results with less effort (only a fool goes the other way as a matter of course), but it has its dangers. The third or fourth time you call back your reprogrammable servitor and give it a job to do, you may well allow it more freedom, infuse it with more chaos, so that it can make decisions for you and get the job done without pestering you for further instructions. You have promoted it from slave to undermanager. You got what your laziness wanted, and it got more complexity, more chaos. Everybody's happy, until you do this one time too many, and find yourself in dialogue with it, with it attempting to advise you—something which was definitely not in the original deal.

It may attempt to gain more power by advising you to use it more often. For instance, I finally banished one egregore entity when it tried to convince me that I should use it when driving, to clear roads, protect my car, etc. Eventually I realised that I was almost continually using it to remove the most trivial obstacles, and I dismissed it and constructed some far simpler servitors for the separate tasks I still wished to perform.

Now a tulpa is a type of entity that can exist independently of the magician's will to a large extent. Whilst created by a magician or group of magicians in the first place, its creators infused it with far more degrees of freedom, instilled more primal chaos into its structure. The working which created it may have utilized random procedures, like cut up text, action painting or collage. At core, a tulpa is highly chaotic. It may appear in the spirit vision as an entity almost bursting the limits of its form, its outer envelope shot through with cracks from which pour the black radiance of chaos. It is far more 'intelligent', powerful and dangerous than an ordinary servitor.

Fortunately for us, humans are capable of accessing even more chaotic and extreme modes of being. The human form is forgotten in moments of wild ecstasy, warping into something that can control by sheer will any human created entity, can subdue it by a vast access to chaos. In my experience, humans are more chaotic, intelligent, powerful, free and dangerous than any such being.

The fact that most of our species choose not to be, far from negates the experience of the sorcerer. It merely confirms magic as an elite preoccupation.

From Issue 18: Catching an Astral Dose

Reading the title of this piece, and some of the contents, is a bit cringe-making. I was obviously wanting to cause offence.

But I'm presently OK about being rude about some people's beliefs. At the time it was just a visceral distaste for the sloppiness of New Age thinking, but these days the New Age is now confirming all my old suspicions and worse: the grotesque overlap with QAnon, the far-right fantasists who put the 'con' in 'conspirituality'. The ultra-right found ways to infiltrate the consciousness of fluffy hippies, and this is possible because their victims are people who, whilst moving into magical thinking have suppressed their critical faculties, so they'll believe anything that offers sufficient emotional reward.

People in that position are being exploited by extraordinarily sophisticated propaganda organizations, who are working for the ultra-right or possibly foreign governments doing anything they can to destabilize the USA or EU. QAnon hooks people in because it is a LARP. This is a new way to do propaganda and it's very clever, and obviously designed by gamers. The designers realised that by using an idea everyone can get behind—child abuse is horrible and terribly wrong—they can draw lots of people into an exciting game who'd never normally give their propaganda a second glance. Then those people dig themselves in further by 'doing research'—i.e. watching YouTube videos from the same lie-factories, and get rewarded with social approval for their 'research'.

The mental processes of so-called conspiracy thinking are identical to early phases of magical consciousness. We have to be outside of mainstream reality in order to function as magicians, so denial as an early stage of breaking out of conventional reality is also a feature of the early stages of becoming a magician. In my teens, one of the things that nurtured my growing magical consciousness was a denialist bit of graffiti: *REALITY IS A RIP-OFF*.

But there's a gulf between QAnoners and magicians. The former lack any critical perspective regarding their exit from mainstream reality and are so heavily emotionally invested in their worlds that they don't want that perspective, they don't want to be aware.

This is a refusal to practice mental hygiene. For such entrants into magical thinking, 'New Age' rhymes with 'sewage.' But somehow we have got to learn to live with these esoteric soap dodgers. This mess is not going to go away in the near future. The old reality principle of God has been dead for a long time and the newer one of absolute belief in Scientism is not looking too good either. The old world has melted down and it hasn't yet recast itself into a new collective viewpoint. What we have at the moment is what that two-millennium old experiment called democracy is looking like in the early years of the Aeon of Horus, God of War and Vengeance.

But magic can help. What we need is the all-realities approach first articulated by RAW and which became perhaps the deepest part of the DNA of chaos magic practice. We need to practice multi-model thinking, but of course with due care to remain open to awe and undefinable ecstasy. For a longer consideration of these issues, see my forthcoming article for *Fenris Wolf* Issue 12.[17]

[17] *Fenriswolf 12*, no publication date at time of writing.

CATCHING AN ASTRAL DOSE: WORDVIRUSES AND MAGICAL STUPIDITY

Do you ever get sick of some of the drivel talked even by apparently experienced magicians? When an absolute tyro asks you about the distinction between Black and White Magic, or Is The Astral Plane Real? (Yes, and for a small fee I'll reserve you a seat on it), it's to be expected. An enormous amount of shite has been written about magic over the centuries (much of it in the last 30 years), so it's not surprising that some of it rubs off on the newcomer. But when someone with years of magical experience who should know better starts drivelling on about Oh No They've Got the Pentagrams Upside Down, They Must Be Doing Evil Magic (exemplified at a major gathering of magicians 2 years ago), I tend to reach one of two conclusions:

1. The unfortunate person is suffering from temporarily poor judgment, no doubt due to personal problems, intense emotional involvement in the particular issue in question, or accumulation of toxins in the brain. He is probably an unwilling host of stupid wordviruses, and I shall give him another chance in the hope that he comes to his senses.

2. The author of these comments is willingly renting personal cyberspace to these low-grade parasitic notions, and probably being paid in the coin of snug security inside some fuckwit paradigm of personal salvation.

In the latter case, if it is someone whom you have been in contact with for some time, and this type of attitude seems out of place in their behavioural repertoire, and persists, I would recommend the following course of action:

a) Close all remaining deals as soon as possible. It's just possible this person could go spectacularly nova, especially if he is the host of a virus that tells him he is the Great White Astral Knight of the Zilth Panjandrum, come to save Earth And All The Dolphins Too. White Light burnouts are often really nasty; the last case of this kind that came into my view ended up being convicted of child molesting. At least get all your books back.

(A note on 'Satanic' casualties: the variety most commonly encountered is the Satanic Wimp, the kind of person who thinks Boyd Rice is never joking. The worst they usually subject you to is an hour of death thrash music and feeble excuses as to why they can't make it to a meeting/can't handle groups of people/can't afford the bus fare. Their conversations, when articulate, are usually about eliminating inferior people. Basically sympathetic to this notion, you ransack your memory for a meeting with someone inferior to this sad social retard.)

b) Don't have sex with the host again, however good it was. Some wordviruses are actively vampiric, establishing energy dependence, and some gimmick for attracting a donor, in the host. Let alone never seeing your signed first edition of *Liber Null* again, you may well end up sufficiently debilitated to be influenced by, and thereby used as a channel for, the virus. (Such entities sometimes choose to manipulate an individual who is close to the host, but not good host material, so that they can use this person as an 'additional limb', or 'sense organ', or defender of the host. This is of a piece with the behaviour of the Heroin Demon, as expounded in Hannibal the Cannibal's 'Demons Among Us', *CI 17*).

c) Study the behaviour of the suspected host from a distance. A magician cannot afford to let the opportunity slip by to see a different kind of power in action. Don't get drawn into a dialogue with the wordvirus/demon. (As William Burroughs puts it, 'Never proffer sympathy to the mentally ill; it is a bottomless pit'). If you still care for the host, stay in touch as far as possible without allowing your personal boundaries to be breached. In other words, don't compromise about your objectives at any point. Get your books back.

What can be done? A good idea might be to pre-empt the appearance of dangerous and stupid word viruses by listing them. A sort of modern demonology. As a contribution, the following list is offered as a suggested study course in GCSE Magic:

1. Pentagrams: Which way up should they be?

2. Black and White Magic: Whose side are you on?

3. Basic Correspondences: Will it produce evil effects if my Jupiter incense turns out pink?

4. The Astral Plane: Can I get trapped on it? Could I bring back vampires, succubi, incubi, etc? (Yes, but go early and get a pretty one)

5. Psychic Attack: Why me? (Because you're so important to the Fate of the Cosmos)

6. An It Harm None: (Can I sell you some Karmic Insurance?)

7. Polarity: Is it possible to do sex magic if you're not a heterosexual couple? (Yes, but only if you're not trying to Save the World. THAT sort of magic is for Properly Polarized Priest/Priestess Soulmate Pairs only. What a relief).

8. My Clairvoyant Perception of a Symbol: 'People who meditated upon the Chaos Sigil got their power sucked out!' (Congratulations! Give yourself due credit for creating that reality!) Actually, this is a particularly pernicious arena of wordvirus activity. Examples crop up even in the most exalted magical circles.

9. Animal Sacrifice: help, my chicken's stopped squawking!

10. 'There are immortal adepts in the Himalayas who can levitate and do anything!' (Probably true.)

11. 'GAIA doesn't like Chaos Magic/Black Magic because it doesn't put peaceful vibes into the Earth' (GAIA can shrug and hurl us off Her shoulders any time She pleases. As far as I can work out, if Gaia has any plan at all, it favours the bold and intelligent. I suspect She enjoys the entertainment.)

12. 'My High Priest/High Priestess said her contacts said it was Evil!' (Ask your HP if it isn't about time they grew up and took responsibility for their own moral prejudices and stopped projecting them onto poor helpless extraterrestrials and discarnate Adepts who can't answer back.)

OK, so I've been blowing off steam. Look a little closer, though; let the boundaries of your thoughts loosen, fall apart. Your own mind is a colony of wordviruses. Each is a collage of ancient meanings, atavistic memes, each in themselves built up from shapes and sounds, the primal phonemes of the primate hunting group, the cries of babies.

These structures form the content of all your thoughts and ideas. Not only does it appear that there is no means of communication other than the virus medium of words, so it can also be seen that identity itself is a colony of these viral structures. There is only Mind (or No Mind, Sunya, Chaos) and its Contents (Rupa, Symbols). There are no other options than to assimilate, understand, feel, be engrossed in the modality of the word. In the beginning was the Word, and the Word was Virus.

The pursuit of magic involves the decoding of your trigger memes, the wordviruses that have real power (negative or positive) for you. Automatic responses are the chinks in a magician's armour. Investigate all your most loaded concepts. Observe the tunes to which your behaviour dances, the drumbeat you march to. Adopt wordviruses that are novel for you, in the form of statements, and feel what it is like to invest them with belief. Eventually you should reach a level where the remaining memes are extremely powerful and lodged firmly in your behaviour.

These structures are the core patterns of your selves. In a negative context, you could say they were your great personal demons. On the other hand, they are great sources of power—it is just that their nature is inherently conservative, being of the viral nature of Word, always seeking to replicate itself intact.

Working with these personality patterns is beyond the scope of this article. The point is, Words Have Power, and a magician prefers to wield that power, rather than be controlled by it. The latter option is the essence of much that passes for magical thought, and the results are all too obvious.

From Issue 20: Magic and NLP

I went off NLP. Like all heavily marketed schemes, it promises a lot more than it usually delivers.

But it does have some useful techniques and approaches, which I've assimilated into my own work and still use, not to mention the therapeutically valuable practices. And it really does have some interesting parallels with magical techniques which made me rethink some of my magical ideas, and that's always a good thing.

In point 5, 'Congruence', I quote a study of communication which has been widely rejected. The rest of the argument stands, though.

MAGIC AND NLP

INTRODUCTION

NLP, or Neuro-Linguistic Programming, has been described as the art and science of excellence. It consists of an ever-expanding set of techniques designed to increase personal effectiveness. Its practitioners claim that NLP studies 'how we do what we do', and 'how we can do it better'. The origins of NLP lie in the work of Gregory Bateson, an anthropologist and writer on communication and systems theory, and the pioneering studies of Richard Bandler and John Grinder, a psychologist and a linguist respectively.

Initially, Bandler and Grinder were interested in how the tiny number of really effective psychotherapists actually got the results they did. They produced models of the practices of three successful therapists. These three used very different approaches, but Bandler and Grinder discovered surprisingly similar underlying patterns in their work. They looked at these patterns themselves, and produced the first NLP model, which they began to apply to enhance communication, personal change, accelerated learning and increased life-quality. Their own view of the power of these techniques is reflected in the titles of their first volumes *The Structure of Magic 1* and *2.*[18]

That was back in 1975–77. Now, NLP is used in training therapists, in sales training, in a wide variety of educational situations (training riflemen, for instance), and hypnotism. My experience suggests that magicians can also benefit from its techniques.

NLP TECHNIQUES

I have chosen a few techniques that are particularly relevant to magicians. There are many more.

1. Sensory Acuity

This is a basic module in most NLP courses, because a lot of the other techniques rely on it. It consists of a fine-tuning of your sensory awareness so that you notice more how people change from second to second. It enables you to monitor (with occasionally astonishing accuracy) what someone else is experiencing. One application of this is to notice how someone is responding to an idea you present.

The elements of sensory acuity include noticing:

a) Skin colour variations

---

[18] Grinder J, & Bandler R (1989). *The Structure of Magic 1: A Book About Language and Therapy*, Science and Behavior Books.

b) Skin tonus variations—changes in facial muscle tone and degree of shininess of the skin

c) Lower lip size

d) Pupil dilation

e) Changes in depth of breathing

f) Changes in voice tone

etc., etc.

Sensory acuity can be trained with the following exercise:

Take a partner, preferably not someone you know in great detail. Sit facing him or her in good light, and look at his face. Make mental notes of the features you notice—i.e. take a 'snapshot' of the person's face. Now say to him 'Think of someone you like'. Observe the changes in his face; the feeling he is experiencing will probably take a few seconds to consolidate, and then begin to fade away. Take a 'snapshot' of the changed face. Now say 'Think of someone you don't like', and make the same observations, take another snapshot. A practitioner would say that you have 'calibrated' this change.

Now comes the interesting bit. Say to him 'Think of the person of those two who lives nearer to you' (or 'who has longer hair'—any neutral descriptive element), and watch his face change. It will probably take only a few tries at this before you are able to identify whether he was thinking of the liked or disliked person.

2. Rapport, Matching, Pacing and Leading

Rapport is an important element in communication. It is refined through sensory acuity, and expressed through matching. Matching is the mirroring of another person's body language. For instance, if you are negotiating with someone, notice what she is doing with her face and body, and begin to practise matching the movements. If she has her legs crossed, you might cross yours. If she is using one of her hands to gesture near her face, you might raise your forearm and mirror the approximate positioning of her hand.

Matching is a delicate skill—if done clumsily, it can look like mimicry and widen the gulf between you and the other person. When done well, it sends out a message of rapport at an unconscious level, which eases the flow of communication.

Pacing and leading is a dynamic variant of the same procedure. A good example would be an argument, where your antagonist is much more wound up than you, performing angry gestures, talking loud and fast, breathing fast. Let us say that your objective is to bring the argument onto a less emotional level and work things out. Your tactics might work as follows: Pace him, by matching his voice and gestures, but with the edge taken off: you don't want to escalate the argument by shouting back.

Your training in sensory acuity will help you decide when rapport has been achieved. When you have achieved the match, gradually wind down the intensity of your voice and gestures, at the same time introducing the points you want to be heard.

3. Anchoring

A very powerful tool that relies heavily on sensory acuity is the 'anchoring' of emotional/physiological states to a chosen trigger. This is in fact a very precise form of emotional engineering, or self-evocation. Helping a client set an anchor follows these basic steps:

a) The client decides what emotional resource he wants to have at his command. Let us take the example of confidence in social situations. (It is worth noting at this point that the practitioner need know absolutely nothing about the resource your client is working with). The client gets ready to recall a past vivid experience of this emotion.

b) The client recalls the experience whilst the practitioner watches carefully, calibrating the 'curve' of the emotion to the appearance of the client—i.e. watching the emotion build, peak and decay. The practitioner remembers the timescale of the emotion, so that he knows how many seconds from start to peak.

c) The practitioner gets the client to 'break state', by talking about the weather, football, whatever.

d) The client recalls the emotion again, and, when the practitioner thinks it is peaking, he touches the client. A brief, firm touch on the arm would be typical.

e) Hopefully, the client now has the emotion anchored to the external stimulus, the practitioner's touch. In order to test that the anchor has 'taken', the practitioner breaks the client's state again, then 'fires the anchor' by the same touch, watching the client carefully. If the client appears to be experiencing the desired emotion, and reports as much, the anchor has taken. If not, repeat steps b) to d).

f) Now we need to anchor the emotion to the client's internal system (since the practitioner isn't always going to be there to help him set off the anchor). This is done by getting the client to decide on his own stimulus—screwing up his toes would be an example—then doing step d) again. Only this time, as the practitioner touches the client, the client fires his own stimulus. Again, test the degree of anchoring, and repeat if necessary.

4. Well-Formed Outcomes

Goals are more likely to be achieved if they are:

a) Stated in the positive;

- i.e.: What do I want?

b) Placed in appropriate context;

- When, where and with whom do I want this?

c) Expressed in sensory specific form;

- What will I see, hear and feel when I have achieved this outcome?

d) Initiated and maintained by self;

- Is there anything in the world that is standing in the way of my getting my goal?

- Am I in charge of all the changes required?

e) Preserving the positive aspects of the present state;

- Will I lose anything I have now by gaining this goal? And if so, do I value what I lose?

f) Of appropriate size;

- Is it big enough to motivate me? (Consider making it bigger)

- Is it small enough to not seem completely unrealistic? (Consider breaking it down into subsidiary outcomes)

- Is it worth the effort I shall need to put into it?

g) Having positive consequences;

- What are the consequences of achieving this goal (for me and any others I consider)?

- How will my life be different?

- Does it fit in with what I am and what I want to become? (values question).

These points are a good structure for clarifying goals, and they help keep you focussed through the process of achieving your goal.

5. Congruence

NLP has been called the martial art of communication. Research done back in the 1960s showed that, in a public presentation, 55% of the impact of the talk was determined by the speaker's body language, 38% by his tone of voice, and only 7% by the verbal content of the presentation. When these three areas are all focussed in the same direction, i.e. congruent, the effect of the speaker is enormously enhanced. This condition borders on to hypnosis, and many hypnotists are NLP trained.

CONCLUSION

So 'Where's the magic?' you say. No circles, triangles, sigils, talismans, robes or altars. But consider how much of the power in the world is wielded by precise knowledge of appropriate techniques for doing your will in the world of human beings. Anton La Vey has a name for this aspect of magic—the Lesser Magic, meaning techniques that achieve willed and apparently marvellous effects without recourse to 'occult' powers. Much of what we want in life can be obtained through the refined application of mundane psychology, and that is what NLP is about.

That was the article as it appeared in *CI 20*. I later added the following further sections as a handout for students on my Arcanorium course *NLP for Magicians:*

EVOCATION & STRATEGIES

One of the most (deservedly) popular methods in the Chaos Magic armoury is the use of servitors. Servitors are instruments, entities with simpler structures than us. We talk about evoking them. They consist of a 'knot' of energy and information with a more or less specific set of instructions to carry out. Generally, as with most magical actions, we don't bother specifying how they will achieve their task, unless to add a few qualifying conditions that stop them taking routes which could cause us problems. The core of a servitor is its set of instructions—to achieve something or other. This will probably have added to it a qualification about when the conditions of the spell are satisfied, when to stop.

This is a very similar structure to the use of Strategies in NLP. A strategy is a set of instructions for getting from one state to another. Those states could be physiological, emotional or mental. Everybody uses strategies. For instance, if you go shopping for a pair of trousers, how do you know when to stop looking and take a particular pair?

Or how many times do you need to test something before you're convinced? The following are a few typical 'convincer' strategies: The 'automatic convincer' has seen proof once, and is now always convinced about this kind of thing. The 'consistent convincer' needs to test the situation every time, every new situation. Another style of convincer has to leave a period of time after the evidence has been presented before becoming convinced.

The underlying psychological model for strategies is the TOTE Model. TOTE stands for Test-Operate-Test-Exit. With the first T, the strategy tests the situation, by matching its internal criteria to what it perceives, and finds the thing it is looking for is missing. So it moves to OPERATE, in other words it carries out its instructions. It then tests again, the second T. If its internal criteria are now satisfied by the available evidence, then the result has been obtained, and it proceeds to EXIT, in other words, stops carrying out its instructions. If the criteria are still unsatisfied, it goes back to OPERATE, carrying out its instructions again. This part of the TOTE cycle loops until the criteria are satisfied.

So, as with a servitor, the strategy is an automated process based on instructions.

Thinking about the nature of what's happening here can lead in interesting directions. 'Proto-NLP' writer Maxwell Maltz, in his book *Psycho-Cybernetics*, describes the action of the subconscious mind as the 'automatic success mechanism'. He points out that the subconscious loves to take on instructions and carry them out, and his book is all about self-programming for self-improvement. This picture of the subconscious is rather like the traditional Norse *hamr*, the soul which shape-shifts, which takes on any form given it.

In Week 3 we worked with the subconscious mind in its mode of providing information, by doing congruence testing. We drew information out of the subconscious, similar to talking to familiar spirits. With strategies, we are putting information in. As with any other intervention in the deeper mind, it helps enormously to ask the subconscious mind whether the proposed intervention is acceptable. We are presenting something new, to an immensely complex system that already has numerous instructions running in it.

These instructions may be conceived of as working in a nested system, with some operating at a higher level than others. Some instructions, such as those that concern survival and other basic needs, will tend to have a more all-encompassing quality, and will be more difficult to modify than more superficial or task-specific instructions. Others will concern complex tasks which, when they are carried out, will require subsidiary instructions to be enacted to support them.

Strategies are built up from tiny but important details of internal representation, what we have already defined as submodalities. To create a strategy, you need to look at the representational systems used—i.e., when you visualize, when you audualize, when you feel feelings and when you get internal monologue. Then you need to look at the fine details, the submodalities, then you need to string together these internal representations into a sequence which will get you the internal state you want.

Let's look at strategies for self-motivation. One person might, for instance, motivate himself to get a task done by looking at the job, hearing a loud, positive voice saying 'Time to get on with this', followed by a big, bright, colourful visualization of the finished job. Looking at this picture makes him feel good, and he starts the task. That sounds like a pleasant and effective strategy.

An ineffective motivational strategy might be as follows: She looks at the job to be done and hears a nagging, unpleasant voice saying 'You should do this'. This produces an unpleasant feeling and a resistance to doing the task, so she makes a big, bright picture of something else she'd prefer to be doing, and feels better. Then, of course, she probably goes with the pleasant picture and does the other, more pleasant task. The original task only gets done after she feels really bad about the consequences of not doing it. That sounds like a less pleasant strategy to run.

Note the structure of those strategies: they both use visualization, internal monologue and feelings.

INVOCATION & MODELLING

Invocation is the 'calling-in' to oneself of some larger system, a God or Goddess. To take a more general, less traditional definition by Pete Carroll: 'the process of invocation may be seen as adding to the magician's psyche any elements that are missing' (*Liber Null*).
Invocation occupies a similar position in magic to modelling in NLP. One of the core presuppositions of NLP is that if one person can do something, it is possible to model it and teach it to others, thereby adding elements to that person's psyche.

Modelling is the basis of NLP, the process of reproducing excellence. It is how NLP got started.

In order to model a skill, you look at 3 levels (Dilts' Neurological Levels):

What the modelled person does—not only their behaviour, but their physical states ('Physiology');

How he or she does it from an internal viewpoint—i.e., the way they think about what they are doing, and

Why he does it—his beliefs and values about the behaviour.

The way you do this is in 3 stages:

Be with the person when they are doing their skill. Observe them. Ask them about it. Become empathic with them, imagine you are them. You will probably find that they know next to nothing about how they acquired the skill, so you are engaged in a process of imaginative archaeological reconstruction of their learning process.

You now have a lot of details, some of which are relevant to the skill, others merely personal to the skilled person and not relevant to anyone else. Systematically remove each element of the person's behaviour and check whether it makes any difference to the results you get when you try it out. Obviously, if it doesn't, you can drop it from the model.

Break down what you have done into a series of steps, so you can teach it to others.

An article about occult modelling in a book I saw briefly many years ago stayed with me. A group of NLP researchers hired for modelling a consistently and impressively successful hands-near healer. They ran seminars around this guy all weekend, and at the end of it, one third of the participants could do extraordinary healing using their hands. Another half could get some success.

One of the interesting features of this work was that the original healer, from a hereditary rural tradition, always got painfully swollen hands after doing the healing. Some of the modellers also got this effect, but they realized that it was not an important feature of the technique, and convinced their subconscious minds that they didn't need the swelling. It went away, and their skills did not. A follow-up study over a year later confirmed that most of the successful modellers could still do the healing.

A challenge to all such approaches is a study reported in the *Journal of Alternative and Complementary Medicine* by a group of Western-educated Turkish doctors. Unfortunately I am still seeking the reference, but the gist of it is as follows: 3 doctors went to a Sufi monastery in Turkey and observed young monks plunging sharp swords right through their abdomens, without any harm at all. We are not talking skin or even muscle piercing here, but avoidance of major organs, the piercing of which would certainly result in death. The most extraordinary thing is that no training is given; the Sheikh of the monastery shakes the hand of the aspirant in front of the community, and that's it, he can go ahead and do the apparently impossible.

What does this mean?

PARTS WORK & MULTIPLE SELVES

Also related to the art of invocation is the chaos magical model of multiple selves, which is shared by some forms of NLP. Bandler himself wrote: 'Evolutionarily, the next step, which we're all engaged in, is multiple personality'.

Bandler also developed the NLP scheme called 'parts work', i.e., treating the different parts of yourself as separate personalities with their own agendas and needs.

A useful concept for parts work, which most people find intuitively obvious, is 'chunking up or down'. Chunking up is taking any category and looking at the next category 'up', i.e., the one that includes it. Of course, there is generally more than one, and may be many, higher categories you can go to. You can chunk a tree up to vegetation in general, then life-forms in general. You can chunk up from a continual desire for chocolate to desire in general, then to the self that desires. Or you could chunk up to security coddling in general, and from there to your security needs. Chunking down is the opposite.

Kaos Magick Journal/Proceedings of the 1994 Thelemic Symposium: Cut up and collage in magic

This piece was first published in the *Proceedings for the Thelemic Symposia* and also a short-run US magazine, *Kaos Magick Journal*. I was honoured to share that issue with William Burroughs. In 1993, as chair of the public chaos magic conference UKAOS, I'd had the honour of announcing that he'd joined the IOT, and didn't mind who knew. My heart swelled with pride! Two parts of my life were coming together!

CUT UP AND COLLAGE IN MAGIC

I've been making collages from newscuttings and magazine pictures for some years. What started out as an amusement I came to realise was a fascinating and powerful magical tool. The first collage I made was made for fun, it was a kind of advert for Chaos Magic. It incorporated (for reasons I don't remember or never made conscious) a newsclipping of Jim and Tammy Bakker, the American evangelists, with the words 'pleased about buggings' around them. The week that I first photocopied the collage it was announced on the news that they had been caught up in some corruption scandal. This was my first hint that collage could be a magical method, even when not consciously applied for magical results.

After this, I began to experiment with deliberate collage magic. The next one I made was part of a magical working involving a number of other people, and we got a positive result. However, it could have been the other work that was done that connected with the result. I had a feeling that the collage in itself would have failed, for the following reason: it was too deliberate and serious, too heavy handed, compared with the lightness of touch of the earlier ones. So, I began to attempt to recapture that lightness. I found the use of advertising slogans helpful, and headlines from tabloid newspapers, because of their incredible superficiality.

An analogous technique is the use of scrapbooks. Many years ago, a magical acquaintance of mine was experimenting with the construction of scrapbooks of pictures which he wanted to be in. His scrapbooks were kept like photograph albums, like a record of a life he had already lived. He achieved a number of positive results with this simple method.

An extension of the collage technique is to use song lyrics as triggers for enchantments. A colleague of mine has developed this into a highly effective sorcery technique. It involves choosing a line from a pop song which represents her intent, then hiding the intention by typing out another line from the same song. This line is introduced into letters and collages which are sent to other people. If the recipient knows the song lyrics, the song will start playing in his head, including the key line. There are other levels of subtlety to this procedure which can be added according to the ingenuity of the operator.

Moving on to sound cut up, I shall let the master himself introduce the techniques. William S Burroughs has released an album called *Breakthrough in Grey Room*, which contains examples of numerous styles of audio cut up. Without the benefit on the page of playing these samples, I shall give a brief list:

1. The intercutting ('drop in technique') of two voices. In this instance, Burroughs and his lover Ian Sommerville make the tape together. This is an example of the kind of cut-up that can be used to forge a bond between

two people, such as a love spell (if you are unwise enough to perform such an inevitably disastrous operation!).

2. Present time exercise: Burroughs reads out a spontaneous description of what he is experiencing at that moment. This tape is then an island in time, which forms the basis for: a) time travel experiments, evoking precise nostalgias of time and place and b) 'dislocation in time' enchantments. In this technique, recordings are made of the target place, then further recordings are made at later dates. Intercutting the different recordings produces a sense of dislocation in time, which Burroughs claims to have used in various successful curses. An example of how such a tape might be used is given in Burroughs's novel *Cities of the Red Night.* Clem Snide the Private Asshole is investigating the disappearance of a boy. He goes to the boy's last apartment, and, whilst spinning the tape randomly back and forth, records ambient sounds doors shutting, taps, toilet flushing and so on. He thereby creates a sound picture of the boy's environment. He takes this home and uses it as a background to an act of sex magic aimed to find the boy.

3. Breaking words down into chaotic sound: the repeated use of cut up and overlay on a tape, or the use of a reel-to-reel machine to 'inch' the tape back and forth across the heads, can produce a complete destruction of the original words. The words are triturated out of existence. Sounds like animal voices, machine noises and so on can result. In my experience, high levels of distortion can produce a similar kind of alienness and destruction of subjectivity. Such tapes can be used for attaining bizarre gnoses for deep trance work.

A variant of these techniques is to employ a fast channel changer on a TV to produce a random picture for divination. I was staying with a friend who had a remote control that would cycle rapidly through the channels whilst the screen remained blank. I focussed on my question, then hit the 'stop' button. The resultant TV sequence proved to be a perfect answer to my question.

The power of cut ups and collages is a subtle, personal art that must be experienced to be appreciated. Try it!

CHAOS
THIS IS WHAT YOU WANT
Laws of science have been rewritten
green stuff
something nobody wants?
Mastering the black arts
It's NEW!
virus cash con-trick
link cash dispensers
Forbidden topics
witchcraft practised between the superpowers
AT LAST YOU CAN SPEAK YOUR MIND!
FISH of the WEEK
Nothing to do with us
Monster bugs thrive
beauty from outer space
THE SAME ANSWER.

أهلا وسهلا
يا جماعة

Part 2: Psychedelia and Embodied Alchemy

To bring together the different strands of my life, of magical structure and psychedelic chaos, meant I had to carve out my own path, become something there were no guidelines for. In fact, the situation was worse than that—as far as I could tell, the majority of people in both camps thought that magic and psychoactives were mutually exclusive. Magicians thought they were tainting the purity of their will if they tripped. Most hippies thought that anyone who didn't just go with the flow, anyone who tried to influence the world via magic, was warping the purity of surrender, was perhaps evil. A more moderate view is that those two sides are the Apollonian and Dionysian dimensions of the magical path—intellectual coherence and cosmological structure versus acknowledging that, at the heart of it, it's unnameable ecstasy. These two directions were a long time in coming together for me, and the process is still happening.

I was just starting to write down my magical experiences during the first stirrings of a psychedelic revival in the 1980s. The first evidence I saw of that revival came from what seems on the face of it an unlikely direction. Alistair and Tanith Livingstone were two punks who launched *Encyclopaedia of Ecstasy* in 1983.[19] Alistair had previously been involved in a punk zine called *Kill Your Pet Puppy; EPI* was perhaps aimed at a different readership.

It was in 1987 that I came across *Encyclopaedia Psychedelica International*. It was a sort of neo-hippie mag that had some significant writers from the old days, such as Neil Oram. I wrote a short piece about my experience of the magic of Phoenix Light, *The Temple in the Squat*, now lost to me. The description went along these lines:

The squat we were living in had started out as a rented house, but the landlord had disappeared, so in some ways it was more of a rented house with nonexistent arrears collection. I managed a few summer months in the front downstairs room then another housemate moved out and I took over his room, which was upstairs, warmer and drier. We cleared my enormous old room out and made it into a temple where we meditated or did Qabalistic pathworkings, or used a Pentagram rite to 'open the Quarters' and just explore magical spaces. After Sorcerer's Apprentice coffee mornings, we

---

[19] Most of *Encyclopaedia of Ecstasy* is available online at: https://killyourpetpuppy.co.uk/news/encyclopaedia-of-ecstacy-fanzine-issues-1-2-3-alternative-sex-fanzine-issue-1/

often invited people back for sessions in our temple. On one of those occasions, we hosted Mike and Marian from Southampton, two magicians who were working with their own unique blend of Qabalistic, Enochian and I Ching astral doorways. In our humble temple, they led a combined Opening of the Quarters. It was the first time I had been so electrified by ceremonial magic. As Mike vibrated the Enochian words over my head, I felt as if I was being filled with radiant, structured energy. I had discovered a new magical experience, and it convinced me there was something very powerful to this mystical post-Dion Fortune stuff. The effects were nearer to the clear phases of psychedelic gnosis than the effects of the early chaos magic work I'd been doing with the first IOT group.

I drafted another piece about magic but discovered that the editor, Fraser Clark, was not generally sympathetic to the magical path. (Maybe we all expected too much from him—after all, this man was a friend of pseudo-hippie billionaire and later NHS-looter Richard Branson.)

Those years marked the beginning of the early psychedelic revival that trailed after the acid house music scene and its use of MDMA. The next stage was the massive surge in interest in the medicinal use of psychedelics in industrial, 'Western' culture. From around 2000 when psilocybin became a medicine of choice for depression for some people, psychedelics were suddenly thrust into the cultural mainstream again.

That movement synergized with the revival of Discordianism, dormant since the late 1980s. As in other scenes where there's been a big time lag between one phase and the next, the survivors of the earlier phase help the new scene develop because they know their way around psychedelic experience and the structure of subcultural scenes—how and maybe why some social structures and some kinds of actions succeed better than others.

I presented some magical workings at the original 2016 Festival 23 and at the one-day event in 2018. These are in *Part 4, Public Workings.*

Beyond Recreation, presented at Head Over Heels

This was a presentation for Donal Ruane's one-day event on psychedelics.[20] It outlines as many different ways people use psychedelics as I could think of, to give an idea of the possibilities opened up by these plants and substances, and considers how that trackless immensity can best be held and nurtured by a ritual structuring of time.

This piece is from the notes I used for the presentation, so it's bare, dense and list-like in places. I'm putting it in first because it was my first formal attempt to answer the question, 'What is tripping for?' while the piece at the end of Part 2 is a more recent attempt to do so.

[20] An account of the day can be found on Donal's website: https://headoverheels.org.uk/events/green-angels-2004/

BEYOND RECREATION: PSYCHEDELICS, RITUAL AND TIME HEAD OVER HEELS, GREEN ANGELS, SOUTHWARK, LONDON, 5TH JUNE 2004

The psychedelic experience challenges us to make better use of its incredible potentials for healing, ecstasy and transformation. Using the techniques of breathwork, energy work, chanting, meditation and magic, how do we create psychedelic rituals for the 21st century?

In this talk I'm going to review some of the ideas and techniques that have accompanied my work with psychedelic sacraments over the last 30 or so years, and draw a few lessons for future practice.

What the title means: Have you ever taken a psychedelic and been struck by a sense of awe at the vast ocean of time that just opens up? Time no longer has a single dimension, once we go beyond the consumerist approach to psychedelics; once we go beyond the idea of entertainment and recreation, how do we fill this time?

People may use psychedelics for fun, but in most cases not many times.

This is the point to make some distinctions about what drugs we are talking about: Some drugs, like alcohol, opiates, cocaine, speed and so forth provide relatively reliable access to particular emotions, and thereby assist in the repression of symptoms of chronic distress.

Psychedelics do not work purely through emotions; they also change sensory perception and ideation and challenge identity profoundly. They often give a rough ride, tearing open emotional depths that may make the psychonaut feel that he is drowning in his own past, or overwhelmed by some external spirit or mental force. They offer fearful, wondrous perspectives; they are more drugs of chaos than drugs of mood. As such, they open up possibilities of profound healing and transformation. They also have less potential to be addictive, because they do not provide a reliable route of escape from pain.

MDMA is considered by some as a psychedelic; I would say it is not, if any meaning is to remain in that term. The drug has the remarkable properties of allowing the deepest and potentially most disturbing insights about one's behaviour and feelings to surface without any sense of threat, and of facilitating empathy. These features speed up the process of emotional healing during psychotherapy by an enormous factor, and earn MDMA the new title of *empathogen*. In recreational use, whilst the first few experiences of MDMA are likely to imprint the user with a new sense of freedom to explore feelings and come out of his shell, further regular use tends to degrade the effects into the mere mood-drug level. Ultimately, with MDMA as with any mood-drug use, the pattern of use becomes a habit, a mere consumerism, just as with booze, junk, cocaine or speed. Habitual E-consumers these days tend to refer to 'pills', demonstrating a rather cynical attitude not only to the purity but even the identity of the drugs they are on.

Psychedelics, on the other hand, are not mood drugs, and therefore by their nature are not generally as habit-forming. LSD and psilocybin can be used recreationally, but at some stage the tripper will find himself plunged into his deep inner worlds, and this doesn't usually work well on the dancefloor.

One thing that everyone who has thought about psychedelic experience must have come across is the idea of Set and Setting. Setting is just the environment, the place. Set is expectations.

In ritual work, Setting is the Temple or Lodge or sacred grove—wherever you work. Set is controlled by Intention, both stated and meditated upon, and symbolized by the furnishings, objects and actions of the ritual.

These are the sets and mental frameworks I have identified myself as having used with psychedelics, in the order I discovered them.

There are 8 of these, and I've numbered them 0–8, because the first one is entertainment, and is not useful as a model for later work, because it is essentially a naïve viewpoint, and therefore inaccessible to experienced psychonauts:

0. No worries

Goal: not explicit. No intention except expansion of experience and fun.

Go out walking, go to concerts or parties.

If any evolution actually happens at this stage, it is because it sneaks up on you from behind and rips your naïve assumptions into pieces.

1. Formless exploration, 'wipeout trips'

Goal: Not explicit. In my case, it amounted to an attempt to recover or attain the ground of being, the completely open, relaxed Self, by dint of doing absolutely nothing—which usually meant lying around listening to music.

In this model, one has faith in the ability of psychedelics to change one's life, maybe illuminate one. This was a big chunk of the mindset of the Sixties psychedelic revolution. This is psychedelic punk mysticism, freakdom. Its influences include Leary, but more so Ken Kesey, in retrospect.

In the late 1960s I found that there was virtually no care or concern for each other in such tripping groups (I hesitate the use the word 'communities'). There was a strong element of macho hippy stuff, drawing on phrases from Kesey like 'Never trust a Prankster'. The message is: sort your own stuff out or fall by the wayside.

2. Sex

Goal: Ecstasy; bonding; totally positive emotional state; boundary dissolution, exchange or merging of subjectivity.

Obviously, not a set which is easily adapted for group work.

3. Ritual magick; using low dosages combined with other techniques

Goals: Group mind entity formation (such as in the Chaos group, 1984–87). Oracular experience. Deep spiritual healing. Physical healing. Self-empowerment.

The intentions here are convergent: there is a definite, explicit goal for each ritual.

A notable series of rituals that were incredibly successful were based around the club scene; a friend and magical co-worker, fed up with losing his friends to AIDS, arranged the series as part of an assault on the HIV virus and the AIDS syndrome. With the club owner's permission we would arrive at the club before the start of the main evening's festivities, create it as a sacred space with our initial ritual—using for instance a sigil in flour on the floor, then withdraw to change into ordinary clubbing gear for a few hours. At the end of the night, we would reappear briefly on the dance floor in robes again. We were using the energies of psychedelics, dance and music, channeling some of the ecstasy of the rave into magickal effect. The results were truly impressive, including major remissions in individuals known to the team and an overall shift in how people viewed AIDS: no longer is it necessarily a death sentence, and I believe our work contributed to that shift of perception.

In further ritual workings with and without psychedelics my co-workers and I have increasingly made use of what I shall call the group-energy effect. In its simplest form, this is the witches' Cone of Power, a spinning vortex of creative energy used to empower spells. It is also visible—literally, sometimes—in group breathwork sessions. When I've taught breathwork here in this space, on a few occasions people have opened their eyes and reported seeing auras and energy flows around the circle.

This effect is exploited in George Pennington's 'Breath of Light' to do healing.

In my groups we have sought to structure it more. We have generated flows into the centre of a circle to heal a particular person, around the circle to pass the energy through everyone, in lines that intersect, in pairs that then flow together to a common focus, amongst other arrangements. I thought we were the only people doing this until I saw a painting by Pablo Ameringo, the Peruvian visionary artist, in which four people are drinking ayahuasca in a circle. Two of them are men, two are women, two face into the centre, two outwards. Around them is a torus, a doughnut shaped structure, made of fine filigrees of light such as are typical of

DMT hallucinations. In the centre of the circle are descending a group of incredible quasi-human entities, as if the vortex is drawing them in from cosmic space. I had seen something almost identical to this vision three years before when working with an experimental ritual group. I have since learned that some groups within the Santo Daime church employ geometrical arrangements of human energies for directed healing, and I shall mention this again later.

4. Psychogeography, dérive, drift

Goal: semi-explicit: losing one's boundaries in a natural setting; landscape mysticism.

Culminating in Avebury pilgrimage, 1995.

Not a suitable model for groups other than very small and close ones in relatively 'safe' places.

5. Breathwork sessions, in the style of Stanislav Grof

Goals: emotional healing and transpersonal ecstasy.

With close friend, 1998–2000.

6. Daime church

Goal: self-healing

celebration of higher consciousness

- Within a religious frame, involving:

- strengthening of church egregore and its belief-memes for its particular purposes

Techniques:

Physical arrangement—men at one end, women at the other, musicians and altar in the middle

Singing, hymns

Dancing

Religious icons, images

A tradition passed on by officers of the church

7. Present experimental phase—solitary or with single partner

Goals: Healing and Higher consciousness: the experience of states that are not afflicted by death.

The framework is a synthesis of shamanic, western alternative healing and western magick, perhaps converging towards the concept of the mystery school.

The techniques include:

Banishing rituals to create a sacred space

Chanting, galdor, mantra

Breathwork, often combined with chanting to bring about the Witness state of meditation

8. Where can we go with ritual from here?

Goals: Healing, both emotional and physical;

A spiritual group experience not contained within a specific religious current;

Higher consciousness: the experience of states that are not afflicted by death.

And how are we going to achieve these goals, knowing what we know now?

Firstly, I think we need **two types of Groups**.

Initially, with the primary group, we work in a most general way.

Our objectives are just as above—higher consciousness and healing, the group experience of unmediated spiritual reality.

It is obvious to me that such a group operates by invitation only; it is an enormous responsibility for everyone involved, and each group needs to be sure that the people involved are capable of following some basic ground rules for the sake of all participants.

The second type of group already exists, from time to time, evolving at present out of experimental magickal groups. It could also evolve out of the primary psychedelic group. Either way, it consists entirely of experienced psychonauts.

This group would have as its goals more intensely focused healing work, using the Group Energy effect.

It would use some of the techniques I'm about to outline for the primary group, plus others which work directly on the energy body, the chi or önd, such as Breathwork and Chi Kung moves.

To come back to the primary group, what ritual elements do we need?

0. Maybe some preparatory work: like ayahuasca dieting, fasting, daily meditation, sexual abstinence where appropriate.

Possible sequence on the day:

1. Preliminary discussion and negotiation if it is a group session. Decide on theme, if any, and ground rules. Can use Mind-Mapping to stimulate creative thinking.

2. Prepare sacred space: Can use a banishing ritual if desired. May acknowledge the ancestors, healing spirits, spirits of place—maybe by some object that represents them.

3. May state Intentions out loud, but not necessarily so. This may be interwoven with:

4. Initial purification of participants, for instance smudging/censing

5. The exaltation stage: No mundane conversation. Singing/ chanting. Breathwork. Silent meditation. Prayer. Healing work.

6. Release and grounding: at the end: all participants, especially the more experienced, check that everyone is OK before breaking up the group/circle for the night. Food and drink is a very good idea.

To get into a bit more detail about the techniques mentioned above:

Setting of the place: semiotic signals, charged glyphs.

Imagination, creative visualization.

Chanting: galdor, icaros, hymns— which can lead to development of the witness-self, like in meditation.

Prayer—redefined—in the sense of reaching out into the universal field of information for new software.

*

Anyone who'd like to read a lot more about techniques, interpretations, experience and more in the area of breathwork, energy work and psychedelia might enjoy my book *Life Force*.[21]

---

[21] Lee D. (2017). *Life Force: Sensed Energy in Breathwork, Psychedelia and Chaos Magic*, The Universe Machine.

Head magazine: 'Trance Out'

The trance techno scene, Goa then Psytrance, had been going for some years when I wrote this piece. It already had its own culture, and the magazine *Head*, (which by the names of some of the people involved, which were prefaced with 'Eden', was clearly influenced by TOPY, Genesis P. Orridge's 'Temple of Psychick Youth'), formed a bridge between that subculture and existing esoteric culture.

The psytrance scene is a specialized offshoot of the Western, post-Sixties psychedelic culture which has inherited many of its earlier ideas. It's a peculiar offshoot in that not all psytrancers like psychedelics. In 2019 I was invited to present something magical at the gigantic Ozora psytrance festival in Hungary. I chose to do a workshop on 'Psychedelics and Magical Energy'. My previous exposure to psytrance was two parties in the late 1990s/early noughties, where no-one was interested in psychedelics at all, only in pills and coke and squabbling over nitrous oxide hits. So I hesitated when I was invited to speak at Ozora, but not for long, because it did sound like something better than that.

And it was. My workshop was a total blast, people really working up an energy-magic sweat in the over 30°C heat, and getting results straightaway. We had a great few days, looked after by very kind hosts, and it begins to occur to me that the best way to understand the psytrance scene is that it's a church. Its sacrament is the limiting, enclosing blanket of the relentless monobeat and the way it constrains and tames the wildness of psychedelics; the collective ecstasy is signalled by people raising their hands at the climaxes of the music; its creed is caring and inclusive (insofar as any church can be inclusive), and its faith is that its beliefs are better for the world than the dominant ones out there.

I never did well with churches, and psytrance dancing is too High Church for me—too prescriptive in its approach to gnosis. However, it was nice to worship with this congregation for a few days. And it's a nice congregation; it seems we humans can't help but do religion, and it occurred to me that this is one of the better ones.

It's a very large, worldwide subculture, and it overlaps culturally with magical practice, various shades of activism and self-help health, but also with all sorts of New Age speculations. This is where its edges get dodgy, that uncritical 'I Want To Believe' drive without critical perspective, as I go into under *Catching An Astral Dose* in Part 1.

TRANCE OUT

We are all in trance most of the time. Trance is the energy-saving mode of the brain, the central nervous system's equivalent of an eco-friendly wash cycle. In trance, some cognitive faculties—such as critical thinking, accurate recall and decision-making—are performed less effectively or not at all. Others are enabled: learning is accelerated and smoother. Some exotic states of consciousness, and some magickal abilities may only be accessible in specialized trances.

Anyone who has ever learned a new skill, or overcome an emotional problem or habit knows how to break a trance and form a new one.

A model of learning employed in Neuro-Linguistic Programming states that, when we wish to learn something, let's say driving a car, we start from a condition of not only not knowing how to do it, but also not really knowing the details of what we can't yet do. This is called ***unconscious incompetence.*** Then, when we start learning, when we find ourselves in the abject panic of failed clutch control, we become intensely aware of what we cannot yet do smoothly. This is ***conscious incompetence.*** We then pull the car out of its nosedive into a busy stream of traffic, breathe a sigh of relief, and acknowledge that we have achieved something. This is ***conscious competence.*** We pay for this in a lot of stress. This is an extreme energy-burning mode of consciousness. When we have gone through this process enough times, we stop getting stressed out, and it gets to be easy, commonplace, mundane. We can drive whilst listening to crazy music, holding a conversation and rolling a cigarette, all at the same time. The process of driving no longer occupies our conscious attention. We have achieved ***unconscious competence.***

Now think about this process in terms of trance: let us postulate that initially, we are in a trance in which we cannot drive. Our objective is to achieve a trance in which we can drive, effortlessly, reserving our conscious attention for more important things, like the actual traffic situation. So we shift from one trance to another. The stressful process in between these two relatively easy states involves breaking one trance and creating another. The process can be summed up as:

Unconscious competence —> break trance —> conscious incompetence —> repeat and practice, break trance, make trance —> conscious competence —> make trance —> unconscious competence.

I chose driving for this example because it was one of the most high-energy learning experiences of my life. We all have a lot of energy invested in the trance loops that sustain our current, unconsciously incompetent conditions. It takes a lot of energy to break these.

Anyone who has done any self-change work is likely to be aware that, in order to get results and fulfil your potential, you have to do things you don't initially like—you have to break out of your 'comfort zone', in order to change. To rephrase a popular slogan: 'No pain, no change'. So why do people, including many magicians, put up with so much mediocrity and unhappiness? We prefer to repeat comfortable and familiar thoughts, even if they make us unhappy, rather than strike out into new thought patterns which would make us feel better; we tend to repeat familiar actions which have become ineffective rather than adopt new and more powerful strategies. Psychologists have estimated that 90% of today's thoughts are an exact replay of the previous day's thoughts.

This conservatism of the mind arises from its habit-forming faculty. Any behaviour that is repeated a lot becomes a habit; the mind has learned how to do something one way, and it finds it works, so it keeps on doing it that way. Eventually, the mind no longer thinks about the behaviour at all—it is repeated without any conscious thought. This works well for skills like driving a car—habitual, unconscious competence is precisely what learners aim for. Assuming that the patterns that were learned in the course of driving instruction are effective ones, it is unlikely that one's driving skill will ever need to be radically overhauled.

However, the same forces restrict us in areas of life where more flexibility is desirable.

Our consciousness hardware is programmed to work in two basic modes:

Energy saving: this is the trance and habit mode. Trance and habit have similar structures: trance saves energy by repetition, mental habituation. Habit is physical trance, unquestioning repetitive activity. Conditioned reflex loops are the unconscious equivalent of trance, repetitious behaviours that are embedded below the level of awareness, directly into muscle and nerve. On the level of mental processes, trance-like repetitions of thoughts may trigger associated behaviours, or sustain existing behaviours. This mode of neural activity is non-adaptive, not responding well to new inputs.

The adaptive mode of neural activity is energy-spending. Breaking trance uses a lot of energy, but enables us to re-tool our skills for new situations.

These modes are complementary: they are the *Solve et Coagula* of the alchemical formula. The trance-habit mode reflects the natural urge of all beings to move along the path of least resistance; without it, relaxation and pleasure would be impossible. The break-trance-adaptation mode exists to enable us to overcome the limitations of our thought patterns and install new, more relevant ones.

It is in the realm of emotions that habits are most obviously troublesome. We all live in our emotional past to varying degrees; all our present feelings are generated by our nervous systems, together with all their past imprints. This means that our responses are refracted through layers of past experiences. In other words, it is very seldom that we live in the present. Since people do more to avoid pain than to obtain pleasure, the tendency is to dampen and reduce all experience. Since all pleasure, all ecstatic experience, is present-centred, it follows that anyone who wishes to live fully and intensely will want to acquire the skill of living emotionally in the present. This is one of the prime reasons for understanding how to make and break trance.

Systems analyst Dennis R. Wier (in *Trance; from magic to technology*; Trans Media Inc., 1996, reviewed by the present author in the last *Head*) adds useful detail to this view of trance. His theory states that when we repeat closed loops of thought, rhythm, music or any other perceived stimulus we get what he calls trance-generating loops or TGLs in the brain. What happens then is that our conscious focus, our attention, gets split, producing a dissociated state. He calls the trancey part of what we focus on the 'dissociated trance plane' or DTP. When sufficient energy is invested in this DTP, then we become separately aware of it, apart from the TGL loop, and our attention has shifted into the DTP. We are then in trance. This theory predicts that some trances, and therefore habits, are very difficult to break. If the energy invested in the TGLs and multiple DTP's exceeds the energy available to the whole bunch of nested loops that makes up the current 'ego', then we are in trouble. In order to break such a trance, we have to shift so much energy out of existing loops that the structure of the current ego is threatened. This can be overcome if energy is made available by disruption of high-energy trance loops, such as happens in intense body-work. Trance induction and hypnotic suggestion can also bypass these blocks.

HYPNOSIS AND TRANCE INDUCTION

The late Milton Erickson is generally acknowledged as one of the great hypnotists/hypnotherapists of all time. Many of the stories told about him concern his ability to enter such a high level of communicational rapport with a client that the verbal instructions he implanted were taken up readily into the client's mind. Erickson was confined to a wheelchair for much of his life, and on one occasion had to deal with a woman who would not let him see her face. He talks with her, and eventually arrives at the key suggestion, implants it, and the client achieves the change she wants. When asked by those who were studying him how he achieved this, he said that he had calibrated to her state by watching a pulse in her ankle.

Normally, the situation is not so difficult, but this story illustrates the importance of paying very close attention to the state of the client in a hypnosis session. You need to learn how to calibrate what you see in his face or body language to his emotional state. This is a major point in hypnotic technique: calibration to the client by intense attention.

Menus of trance-inducing techniques are readily available in books, but a few samples you might watch out for are:

Staring at something until your eyes are tired. This will tend to generate loops, and make you susceptible to suggestion. This is related to the effects of TV.

Thinking of something pleasurable, going into a daydream, makes you susceptible to suggestion.

State interrupt: a classic version of this principle is the following scenario: you are introduced to someone, you shake his right hand. At the beginning of the shake, you raise his hand way out of the way to your left, move in close and whisper a suggestion in his ear. You then resume the handshake. If this is done smoothly enough, the victim may not dare to believe that anything that weird has happened. Also watch Paul McKenna on the TV and note how he gives a sudden, rapid command which is discontinuous from the rest of what he is saying to the victim. (Of course, it's worth bearing in mind with an entertainment-hypnotist, that when he has a willing victim who wants permission from an authority figure to make a prat of himself, the mere giving of the permission will free the person to act differently.)

Speaking quietly so the other person has to get closer and pay more attention. Obviously, this only works if you already have their attention.

These last two examples come down to calibration again: if you haven't judged the person's attention correctly, such techniques simply irritate or alienate. It can be instructive to watch would-be social hypnotists attempting such tactics.

SELF-HYPNOSIS: GETTING INTO A DIALOGUE WITH GREATER MIND

By 'greater mind' I mean the vast areas of potential awareness that exists in the hinterland of the I, the immense shadowland of sentience that some magicians refer to as *fetch* or *fylgia*, and some people refer to as 'the unconscious'. I prefer the vague term 'greater mind' to the vague term 'unconscious mind', because it is by no means unconscious; the normal 'I' is the part that is unconscious of greater mind's activities, having throttled down its range of awareness to focus on survival. This great scope of sentience is not difficult to reach—we just need to relax and be free from interference for a while. When we are relaxed and feel unthreatened, we can engage in a dialogue with greater mind, and seed it with suggestions for the experience we want.

In the following exercises, if you feel more comfortable using the psychological term 'unconscious' in place of 'greater mind', then go ahead; both, and many other terms too, will work. Don't let theory get in the way of experience!

One really useful technique for inner exploration and re-programming through trance is **recognizing congruence signals.** This involves checking for the signals in your body and feelings when you explore an idea; your intuition, once you have learned to listen to it, will provide you with the answers. For a taste of this kind of thing, try the following exercise:

First, think of something you want in your life. Turn it into a definite simple sentence.

Get into a relaxed posture, and ask your greater mind if it's listening (of course it is, but this is a useful protocol for attuning to it): you will probably get a sensation of some kind; this is a congruence signal, a YES. Now repeat to yourself the desire-sentence and tune in to your body and feelings. You may experience a different sensation, which may be an incongruence signal, a NO, or an indication of need for some adjustment in the desire sentence, a YES, BUT.... Experiment with different formulations of the desire-sentence, until you feel a distinct congruence signal, something that undeniably feels like a YES. When you are confident that this is a congruence signal, you will have formulated a congruent desire.

Now you can take this skill and use it to ask greater mind to give you a useful or exotic experience.

Decide what you want from the trance experience. This is your starting point for negotiating with greater mind.

Induce trance: get relaxed; use any technique that works for you. The following are examples:-

Pick something and stare at it until your eyes are tired. / Think of something you like to look at, something you like to listen to. / Let your body relax... close your eyes... you are gazing at a cat's face, and listening to the sound of rain... You are thoroughly relaxed... more and more relaxed... etc., etc.; calibrate to your own feelings.

Ask greater mind: Are you with me? Check for congruence or incongruence signals in your body.

Ask greater mind to create the experience you want;

Now thank your greater mind, and let it create the experience for you.

The first time you do such an experiment it is useful to have a partner, who will talk you through the trance-induction.

If you persist with such techniques, it becomes rather like dowsing, and is a powerful tool for magick, because you have at your disposal the wisdom of all the levels beyond the conscious mind whenever you want to clarify your will. The fact that you are inviting greater mind to express itself will result in a considerable strengthening of one's intuition. It becomes increasingly possible to steer one's life by the 'feel' of situations—all the information about any decision is present in the feelings of the body, if one can only learn to interpret and trust them.

MAGICKAL TRANCES

In the Viking Age tale *Egil's Saga*, the sorcerer Egil Skallagrimsson finds himself drinking with a roomful of his mortal enemies. He is offered a horn of beer which he suspects is poisoned. He takes his dagger, slashes his hand, carves runes on the horn and stains them with his blood, then activates the spell with a poem: 'I carve a rune on the horn / I redden the spell in blood / these words I choose for your ears'. The horn shatters and the beer spills. He then has to fight his way out of the house, which he achieves. This is a powerful example of what Dennis Wier (op. cit.) defines as a *centric trance*. A CT is the kind of state that empowers the religious lunatic, some forms of sociopath, and the charismatic guru. It is also the trance *par excellence* of intense magickal work, when the delusions present in the other examples are absent. The centrically-entranced person is, basically, in another reality, but, in the case of the magician, is capable of functioning from it. The effect on the inner reality of the wizard is total congruence, absolutely no doubt as to the shift in reality that, in her altered world, has effectively already occurred. The outer effect is charismatic; powerful projections of the wizard's reality can influence the reality of others present. Magical groups often 'carry' the less experienced members into gnosis, via the centric trances of more experienced members.

PSYCHEDELICS, TRANCE AND TRANSFORMATION

In the context of an issue on Altered States, it is worth pointing out that there are two types of drugs, one of which assists trance-breaking, the other of which generates habits, literally.

Mood-drugs simply return us to the same experience again and again, or at least promise to. The most inappropriate words ever penned about a drug belong to an old rock song: '*She don't lie, She don't lie, She don't lie, Cocaine...'* This is a species of extreme bullshit: Cocaine is a great example of a delusional, dishonest drug, its regular use achieving nothing but a desire for more, and a reduced intensity of effect. Mood drugs, by their very nature, delude.

A borderline case that illustrates this point further is MDMA. It has been falsely classified by some as a psychedelic; it is not, if any meaning is to remain in that term. The drug has the remarkable properties of allowing the deepest and potentially most disturbing insights about one's behaviour and feelings to surface without any sense of threat, and facilitates empathy. This speeds up the process of emotional healing by an enormous factor. These properties gave rise to a better classification of MDMA as an *empathogen*. The first few experiences of MDMA are likely to imprint the user with a new sense of freedom to explore feelings and come out of his shell, further regular use tends to degrade the effects into the mere mood-drug level. Ultimately, with MDMA as with any mood-drug use, the pattern of use becomes a habit, a mere consumerism, just as with booze, junk, cocaine or speed.

Psychedelics, on the other hand, do not produce predictable or reliable changes in mood, and therefore by their nature are not habit-forming. They act as alchemical solvents, the *solve* of the *solve et coagula* formula. They dissolve boundaries in the psyche, introduce more chaos into the system, allowing more rapid change to occur. An analogy is the energy-barrier in physics, where a particle has to 'jump' over an energy level far greater than the one it will finally settle down into. If a person has the condition described above, in which the amount of energy invested in a trance loop or habit pattern is of the same order as that invested in maintaining his identity, then changing the habit will be very difficult indeed. Wisely used, psychedelics can provide the leg-up to get over the barrier; the comedown then leaves the person in a new trance, with previously troublesome material integrated into functional consciousness. The master of this technology is Stanislav Grof, and anyone interested in the dynamics of spiritual healing and deep change would do well to check his work out.

To sum up, remember that:

Drugs of mood / always delude

Drugs of madness / transform sadness

Enjoy your brain!

Arcanorium handout: Body Alchemy

One of the essential directions in my path was—and still is—the kind of self-undoing practice which leads to emotional wholeness, and sometimes to radical shifts in my ideas about what kind of universe I'm living in. My first encounter with this type of work was of course psychedelics in my teens, but decades later I discovered connected breathwork, thanks to Lionel Snell and my first IOT World Meeting.

Connected breathwork was a revelation for me. I learned that I had a portable, powerful gnosis—breath—and it could lead to integration of my fractured selves. I described it so:

'I lay on the floor of the mediaeval room and breathed as instructed. Within minutes, my fingers began to tingle. In a few more minutes I began to feel like I was awash with energy. I gave myself up to the buzzing sensation which filled me. Some more minutes after that, I was overwhelmed with a flood of emotion. Sensations of loss and sadness, then anger. At first, this felt uncomfortable, even threatening. As the session progressed, my attitude to the emotions shifted: all sense of threat disappeared and I began to experience the feelings as pure sensation, as waves of energy coursing through me.

'At the end of the session, I found myself bewildered and impressed by the power of this technique: how could such a fantastic shift in awareness happen just through breathing??? And I knew, as I sat and thought about what I'd just experienced, that I had released a whole slew of held-in anger, not by acting it out, but simply by letting go, by being there in full awareness, witnessing some wiser part of me process and reframe that pent-up feeling.'

Back home, I found a Rebirthing practitioner in Sheffield and went for a series of sessions over six months. Connected breathwork came into my life during a difficult year; my life had lost its sparkle and vigour. Breathwork sessions opened it all up, like letting air and light into a shuttered, dusty room.

It was so effective that I decided to go in for professional training.

I learned that there are two modern 'lineages' of connected breathwork techniques, both from the early 1970s, one starting with Stanislav Grof's 'Holotropic Breathwork' and the other with Leonard Orr's 'Rebirthing'. Each has parented a number of 'schools' of connected breathwork.

The Rebirthing lineage gave rise to a new development called 'Vivation' by its originators Phil Laut and Jim Leonard. They trained Hilary Newman of London, whose first Vivation Professional Training course in Autumn 1992 I signed up to.

In six weekends over a year I qualified, and we had a graduation party picnic in August 1993 at Oxleas Wood, recently saved from destruction.[22]

This kind of breathwork leads into energy magic, especially energy healing. In the late 1990s I met the Green Angels collective, who had got the use of a substantial building near Borough station in South London. On Wednesday evenings they held healing nights, and I got into going along and learning to adapt my one-to-one Vivation training to group breathwork. The results were great—not only did people enjoy it but there were quite a few spontaneous energy-sensing events—seeing auras, knowing with closed eyes when someone on the other side of a circle had broken hand contact and so on. This was the same period that some IOT people in Vienna were putting together the most innovative magical idea I've come across in my magical life—the chaotron.

The story of all that is in *Life Force*. That book became necessary because the hinterland between breathwork and energy magic had opened up for me and I wanted to join the dots. This is the area I call *body alchemy.*

[22] Oxleas Wood's reprieve from destruction was announced by me as the MC at UKAOS 1993. It was a powerful moment, as so many people there had done magic to save the wood.

BODY ALCHEMY AND THE HEALING SOUL HANDOUT FOR ARCANORIUM COLLEGE COURSE

WHAT IS BODY ALCHEMY?

Poet and writer on the mysteries Peter Redgrove writes, in *The Black Goddess and the Sixth Sense*, that the fact that wart charming sometimes works shows that skin-cell genes can be turned on and off by word of mouth. This has enormous implications for the arts and sciences of healing.

We're all familiar with psychosomatic healing effects; psychosomatic healing is central to all forms of medicine. Even conventional medicine admits to the existence of the Placebo Effect, and makes use of it with the traditional doctor's 'bedside manner', in other words the bag of psychological tricks the doctor uses to help trick the patient into healing himself, which is all that any kind of healer can ever achieve. If an individual is resistant to health because of their own internal mental processes, then the most sophisticated physical medicine in the world will not make a jot of difference.

On the other hand, a positive attitude to healing can produce apparently miraculous cures. The fact that diseases classed by doctors as incurable are often cured illustrates that most people's confidence in their self-healing powers is far below what it need be.

The finding that immune system cells communicate with central nervous system sites was one of the discoveries that narrowed the gap and enabled more materialistic scientists to take the plunge of believing in psychosomatic healing.

A tentative definition: Body Alchemy is the art of 'bending the apparent rules' of biology to your advantage. The body, at any point in time, is the end product of genes plus conditioning plus habits of action and belief which continually impact on our states of health. We are continually making and unmaking our bodies.

SOME OF MY EXPERIENCES

Two anecdotes involving apparent miracles, from many years of practice:

My friend had an inflamed bowel which had recently got much worse. Following intuition, I did a kind of 'psychic surgery', extracting the 'subtle form' of the disease and neutralizing it. After a struggle, the working was totally successful. My friend had a brief crisis later that night, then recovered completely, from a syndrome she'd had for ten years. That was over ten years ago, and apparently the syndrome never came back.

On another occasion, another friend got quite badly burned. At the hospital her right arm was treated for first- and second-degree burns. In a convoluted pattern of human energies and breath, we all poured healing energy into her. The doctor had said that she wouldn't be able to do without a dressing for two weeks, but in less than forty-eight hours she was able to remove the bandages, and a day later the burns had healed without trace.

Both of these were group efforts, and I'll mention more about working in groups later.

WHAT'S GOING ON?

What then is the basis of psychosomatic (i.e. 'magical') healing and body alchemy?

It seems that a will to get better acts via some subconscious instructions to change gene expression. This is the type of mechanism of many traditional forms of healing, of the so-called placebo effect (which is, of course a kind of healing magic), and also feats such as firewalking.

The subconscious mechanism appears to act through a trance, a specialised state of consciousness. This 'healing trance' is used on a daily basis by traditional healers and shamans the world over.

From the inside, experientially, this trance typically has some or all of the following features: A sense of being suspended away from the problems and urgencies of ordinary existence; a feeling of pleasure that is not dependent on sensory stimulation (although it may be enhanced by it); a reduction in the internal monologue, the self-talk we usually engage in.

The latter effect, this inner silence, is the beginning of deeper levels of trance: the experience of doing hands-on (or hands-near) healing is often accompanied by a cessation of the ego's babbling, and a sense of direct connection with the task at hand. (This latter state was named 'flow' by psychologist Mihaly Csikszentmihalyi). Intuition is one's guide as to what action to take; some healers experience this as 'channelling'. This is an important feature I'll come back to.

In this deeper state, there is often a sense that the flesh has become 'light', or 'filled with light', or 'suspended in light', or even that the flesh is no longer 'solid', but 'fluid', mutable, even immortal. The body as process, rather than 'frozen sculpture', as well as a sense you can move energy about, or cooperate with its spontaneous flowing and streaming.

The latter sensation is at the root of some forms of esoteric 'aura' models. In these, the body's cells and organs are viewed as being suspended in a matrix of subtle structure, of 'etheric patterns'. Whilst literal belief in such a model is in no way necessary in using the experience of the trance itself for healing, there is increasing evidence for some form of field around and within biological organisms that is generated by the organism itself and which functions as a long-range structuring device.

EXTREME BODY ALCHEMY

How far can we 'bend the apparent rules' of biology? For a start, it is worth emphasizing that we are talking about apparent rules; as each advance in biological science occurs, like the finding mentioned above that immune system cells connect with the nervous system, this frees up more belief, which empowers us in our healing work. So what are the limits of what we can do with body alchemy?

Perhaps the most impressive demonstrations of the potentials of the body come from martial artists. Healing and the energy-based or 'inner' martial arts have a lot in common, in fact seem to be different uses of the same human potentials.

A friend of mine witnessed at first hand a Shaolin monk from the Hong Kong monastery set fire to paper without the use of matches or a lighter. He was told to arrive at the monastery with a newspaper, and a sizeable donation to the monastery's funds. The monk screwed up the paper into a ball then stared at it until it burst into flames. A similar event was captured in the 1980's TV series 'Ring of Fire', about the adventures of two Brits in the Pacific Islands—an Oceanic shaman was filmed staring at a piece of paper until it caught fire. Both the shaman and the Shaolin monk emphasized that they had to train for years to do this, and prepare for a few days for the event itself, after which they weren't much good for anything for a few more days, having been depleted in some way by this expenditure of energy.

As to what is happening in these cases, there may be a connection between fire-magic and the Chinese observation that Yun-qi healers (who work rather like Reiki practitioners, using hands-near healing) emit a particular, measurable pattern of microwave output from the palms of their hands when, and only when, they are projecting healing energy. Maybe the monk and the shaman were able to project sufficiently intense microwave energy to ignite paper, but we're in the realm of speculation now.

Another extreme form of body alchemy is probably involved in the anecdotes one occasionally hears about a woman or man of average strength lifting up one end of a car in order to save a child trapped underneath it.

METHODS USED IN BODY ALCHEMY

Any technique which helps us to achieve the 'healing trance' can be used as a starting point. Meditative stillness leads to breaks in the internal monologue and the opening-up of the deeper levels. Concentration on energy-exercises such as Qi Gong or Tai Chi brings an awareness of the flow of energy in and around the body.

Sexual alchemy, the transformation of sexual desire and excitation into awareness of energy flows, is a powerful technique (where appropriate!). Psychedelic sacraments, as in the early work of Stanislav Grof, can be used to loosen up the limits of belief and trigger deep transformations, sometimes accompanied by physical healing, though they are usually too disorienting and long-lasting for regular work.

After Grof was forced by changes in the law to cease his therapeutic use of psychoactives, he became (around the same time as, and independently from, Leonard Orr) one of the two (re-) discoverers of connected breathwork, the use of continual, deeper and faster breathing, which produces deep healing states. This process is often experienced as realignment of energy flows and the dissolving of blockages in the energy-system. I shall deal with this in more detail below.

Another important technique used in body alchemy is what we might call the group energy effect.

HEALING ENERGIES IN GROUPS

Some of my most powerful experiences of healing and transformation have occurred in groups. I mention three of these above, but I've also experienced milder but still highly impressive effects when coaching breathwork or receiving breathwork coaching in larger groups.

The style of breathwork I'm qualified to coach is in the lineage of Orr's 'Rebirthing breathwork' and Laut and Leonard's 'Vivation'. These schools tend to work mainly on a one-to-one basis, the coach paying full and empathic attention to the client on their inner adventure, but can also be applied in larger groups, where it is not uncommon for the majority of participants to experience flows of energy, sometimes visible, outside of their own skin and which connect them into greater flows with other participants.

This principle is the basis of a structured use of breath and energy-perception and visualization to entrain flows of energy outside the skin and through other participants, so that the whole group becomes a kind of 'energy collective' for the duration of the work. One of the spectacular effects of this is mentioned above.

These effects are also the basis of the breath circle, brought to prominence by George Pennington's 'Breath of Light' practice. A lengthy and fascinating article about this has unfortunately been removed, but basically it consists of a group of ten or more people lying on their backs with their feet to the centre, holding hands and doing intense breathwork for long periods, up to a few hours.

As the energy flows build up, participants experience some consciousness of the entire circle of people—for instance, it is vividly obvious not only when someone in the circle breaks hand-contact but also where the break is. This is followed by readjustments of blocked flows, energy surpluses (which are easily generated in intense breathwork) flowing into areas of low energy and causing healing. Pennington tells the story of the discovery of the Breath of Light as happening when one of the participants at a weekend healing retreat had waited too long for her dialysis procedure, and had gone into a very scary kidney crisis. People in the group were inspired to form this new arrangement (I go into the idea of a spontaneous sense of guidance below), did so and the sufferer was restored to health for at least long enough to get to her next dialysis without mishap.

Interestingly, the principle of the energy-group and the breath circle must have been known to shamans for years. At least one of the paintings of Pablo Ameringo, Peruvian visionary artist and ex-shaman shows circles of healing surrounded by structured light; clearly the participants have consciously or spontaneously arranged their positions to generate healing flows of energy. (Check out http://headoverheels.org.uk/ especially the painting 'Los Archontes Volares'.)

So what's going on here? Anyone who has experienced such a group healing will be happy to attribute it to what it appears to be—a flowing, a shifting-round of energy between the people in the group.

Reductionist psychologists have another theory, the Large Group Awareness effect. This is encountered in some critiques of NLP, and addresses the fact that the psychological techniques used in that discipline often have more dramatic effects when people go along to a large group as compared to doing the same procedures at home.

This of course is related to the barely controlled ecstatic enthusiasm of religious revival meetings, where apparently miraculous healings sometimes happen, and other collective enthusiasms where religious (or political?) 'conversions' occur. There is clearly some powerful effect going on here, an effect which has potentials both for powerful healing and for deranged, fanatical behaviour when misapplied.

The mechanisms of the 'Large Group Awareness effect' presumably include the fact that everyone in a group is being given permission by everyone else to enter an extraordinary state of consciousness. Social permission is a powerful thing, especially when applied to non-ordinary states.

An example of social permission in action can be found by comparing the methods of Stan Grof's holotropic breathing with the rebirthing-vivation schools of breathwork: Grof's HB is done in large groups—60 breathers plus 60 co-coaches is typical, with loud, rhythmic music on, whilst rebirthing-vivation is usually practiced one-to-one, in a kind of meditative near-silence. The transformations triggered by both kinds of work are comparable, but the spectacle of them is entirely different. A vivation session may occasionally and with some clients, include the client acting out extreme states—laughing, crying, kicking legs out, curling up and so on, but a Grof workshop, with its pounding orchestral or electronic music, seems to give permission for people to act out their energy-transactions in a much more extroverted way—writhing around, leaping up from a prone position, shrieking or going into glossolalia ('speaking in tongues') are typical, and the more you're aware out of the corner of your eye that other people are acting out extreme states, the more you feel you have permission to do likewise.

This is not a criticism of either school of breathwork—both styles are immensely valuable, and given the choice, most people will find that one or the other is more appropriate at the particular stage of their healing process they find themselves at.

The psychological aspects of the group effect are certainly important parts of its mechanism, and admitting a conventional, psychological basis for some aspects of group healing does help it become more 'respectable' to the mainstream and hence practiced more.

However it does appear that, given that initial trigger of group permission, something very special then takes place. Anyone who has experienced group healing at first-hand is likely to look at the energy-transactions themselves as being the things of interest. From the point of view of the healer, the important result is that the healing gets done, not an academically respectable theory of how it gets done, and so the healer will, and should, gravitate towards a belief about what is happening that empowers him or her to heal more effectively.

BREATHWORK AND BODY ALCHEMY

What does breathwork do? Many clients who've failed to find relief with talking therapies and hypnosis find that breathwork is the only thing that really works for anxiety, dealing with stresses of everyday life, insomnia and depression and often report that they 'just feel happier with myself as a person', 'happier, calmer, more self-assured'. (See below for link to reports and discussion of breathwork's effects). Relief of symptoms of psychosomatic complaints are also common, and more rarely, reports of physical healing events.

However, some breathworkers have claimed much more for it—for years Leonard Orr claimed it can bring about physical immortality, and apparently his recent writings still do. Some breathworkers have done a bit of hand-waving about the 'symbolic' nature of immortalist claims, but in an early book by Sondra Ray she is very clear about exactly what physical immortality means: "Physical immortality can be defined as endless existence; specifically, the endless existence of your physical body in perpetual health and youthfulness."

Fortunately, breathwork books tend not to make this claim any more; it does the movement no good at all to be associated with frankly unsupported, cranky ideas.

There is an ethical issue for the coach here too: it is very dubious to present an unsubstantiated possibility as fact, particularly to someone who, perhaps already vulnerable, may take on that belief without question. The client may be trying to please the coach or may lack the self-confidence that would allow them to reject the belief as wrong for them, so for the coach to impose such a belief is very close to the aggressive anti-reason of cultic conversion techniques.

However, the most interesting dimension of the breathwork experience may be the sense of contact with guidance from a deeper layer of selfhood.

THE CORE OF HEALING

The core of the breathwork experience often involves a sense of spontaneous, wordless inner guidance, as mentioned above in the context of the breathwork circle. 'Something' steers us from moment to moment in the way we experience and respond to changes in sensation. Breathworkers speak of a stage in a breathwork session when it is no longer an effort to keep up the unusual breathing pattern and it becomes spontaneous. This is sometimes referred to as 'it breathed me'. This feeling of guidance comes from some part of us that Grof calls the 'holotropic mind', the particular 'soul' within us that seeks wholeness.

This 'soul' draws you into one subtly different way of breathing or moving rather than some other, orchestrating each entry and exit from each stage of the experience and thereby sculpting an adventure in transpersonal consciousness, a journey towards healing and wholeness. It also 'knows' your own rhythm, your own step-style of deep or transpersonal development and decides how fast your liberation can proceed over any given day, week or year.

So what can we say about this 'holotropic mind'? I've been using the word 'soul', and I mean it not in the sense of Christian dogma but in an old, popular sense: that we know we are more than just the conscious data-processing revealed by the internal monologue. We know we have a 'deep mind' that is very hard to touch by any conscious processing, any scheme of thought, however sophisticated, and which communicates with us in ways other than speech.

It was Grof who named this 'soul' in the modern age; presumably, humans have always had such a source of guidance, so we might expect to find a name for it in more traditional systems of healing and soul-lore. Many traditional models of how the human mind works are more sophisticated than the Christian model that has overlaid them. For instance, the ancient Egyptians worked with seven souls, and the ancient Germanic tradition is a very sophisticated one that involves up to nine or more souls.

To clarify this idea of souls and line it up against modern scientific knowledge, it has been said that the human nervous system is rather like a car that took many years to build, so was built in layers, all of which are still present. The chassis is one evolutionary level, the body another, the engine another, the control systems yet another, all built one on top of another. All the ancient layers uncovered by neurology are still with us—the parts we share with reptiles, the parts we share with other mammals, the parts we share with other apes, and the parts that are uniquely human.

The traditional soul-systems give us a means of approaching these non-verbal souls, dealing with the subjective experience of functional layers of human neurology, personifying them as conscious or semi-conscious entities we can engage in dialogue with. As any NLP practitioner can tell you, personification is an extremely powerful way of negotiating between our component selves, based as it is on our most focused and detailed kind of perception—the way we relate to other people.[23]

When we 'talk' to a soul in its own language—which may be symbols, dream-images or bodily sensations—we get useful information back.

In breathwork, the subtle impulses from the 'holotropic soul', that nudge you towards moving in one direction of consciousness rather than another, come through as bodily sensations rather than visual or auditory symbols. The deep processes of breathwork open us directly into dialogue with the 'holotropic soul', via a sense that one way of breathing or moving just feels 'right' or 'better' than some other. Somehow, wisdom arises through the rich continuum of physical sensation and guides us towards wholeness.

This kind of wisdom has been called embodied wisdom, and is recognized as a central component of the more advanced traditional systems of soul-lore. In the Old Norse tales and myths (the Eddas and sagas) we find mentions of a soul that may be identified with the source of this wisdom—the fylgia, for which the English traditional word is Fetch. Ristandi (see reference below) describes some of its functions as follows:

'Although closely connected to the individual, the Fetch possesses autonomous existence... It is a source and repository of transpersonal information. It can guide and advise.'

At the core of the healing experience lies our link with such a deep, verbally-silent part of us.

---

[23] Dukes R. (2005). *Little Book of Demons; The Positive Advantages of the Personification of Life's Problems*, Aeon Books. Also, the work of Phil Farber, http://www.meta-magick.com/

Enriched contact with this 'soul' can only make easier our present and future healing; and more.

In the course of your first few breathwork sessions, there's often a sense that you're beginning to give permission for your deeper mind, your holotropic soul, to communicate more with you. Once started, such a dialogue gets deeper; it gets easier to communicate between the conscious self and the soul that guides. A neurologist might tell us that more connections are being forged between the two sides of the cerebral cortex, more 'wiring' occurring across the corpus callosum. Whatever the physical mechanism, the dialogue gets richer, and a cooperation grows between the conscious self and the mysterious holotropic soul or Fetch. The greater aim of breathwork is, in a sense, to strengthen this link.

And there's more still; this holotropic soul seeks wholeness, completion; my conscious self seeks towards the Other, that which I am not, and which I cannot understand fully at this stage. At some stage, I find I have understood the aspect of it I am looking at, that was a mystery yesterday, but the quest is not over—I move on to a deeper aspect of the same mystery. This process is endless, and the quest forms the core of a meaningful life, of always seeking towards the mystery.

FURTHER READING:

Breathwork: background, practice, coaching and resources: www.chaotopia.co.uk

The Fetch: Ristandi's in-depth study of the practical use of embodied wisdom to work with the Fetch can be found as a free download at: https://www.scribd.com/document/49967333/fetch#

The Mythic Breath, published in Dreamflesh

Gyrus Cope, occultural publisher and writer, has run various journals and online resources. When I first met him, in Leeds in the 1990s, he had a zine called *The Unlimited Dream Company*. Then he created *Towards 2012*, a wide-reaching occultural zine. He's also done some fine Earth Mysteries writings. In 2006 I wrote this piece for his *Dreamflesh Journal,* now located online.[24]

[24] https://dreamflesh.com/projects/journal/

THE MYTHIC BREATH

RENEWING THE WORLD

Perhaps the most outstanding feature of us humans is our adaptive nature, which gives rise to our restless changing. We don't come with a ready-made identity and purpose in the world, but have to make these things up, to make ourselves up again and again, to decide what is real and what matters many times in our lives. On the one hand, we are driven by desire; on the other, by the need to make something of ourselves in the world of humanity. Our desires come into conflict with the inorganic inertia of what is, and the social inertia of what our society demands. As a result, we compromise again and again. This abrasion of the will produces an attrition, which, at worst is weakening and debilitating. As a result, from time to time we need renewing.

However, there is another side to this resistance. Modern culture values individual achievement, the attainment of our desires, so highly that it has long since been forgotten that anything other exists. We get the impression that life consists of the will and desires we carry within us, plus an external universe which is the dead, raw material for their fulfilment. The effects of such thinking on the long-term welfare of the planetary ecosystem, let alone its effects on human social relationships hardly need pointing out to anyone likely to read this. Both as individuals and as a culture we need to rediscover what lies beyond the limits of the self, to look beyond the primal will to survive, to really appreciate that there is something out there. We need reminding that the world outside of us is neither dead nor human-hearted.

Amongst the old Norse tales there is a myth about this attrition, and about renewal, in the image of the world-tree, Yggdrasil. This tree is the heart of the world, weaving from its three roots a triple skein of humans, giants, and the dead. A fierce eagle crowns its branches, a hawk sitting between its piercing eyes. The tree suffers great hardships: The dragon Nidhogg gnaws at it from below, four stags devour its leaves, and the squirrel Ratatosk runs up and down the trunk bearing malicious messages between Nidhogg and the eagle. The Norns, the Wyrd sisters that live by the well, plaster its trunk each day with holy white mud, preserving it against these depredations.

Now might the eagle be the self surveying its world, bothered ceaselessly by the self-talk, the internal dialogue which is Ratatosk? And Nidhogg's unwelcome message, that Ratatosk bears to the Eagle, that gnaws at the root of identity, is the awareness of our own mortality, that our death is scripted in the flesh. And might the gnawing stags be the little losses and defeats, the little deaths that eat away at us in our daily lives?

Against this daily attrition we must work as best we can by daily communion with sacredness, with vital power, taking our cue from the

Norns. We raise up sacred brightness from the deep resources of the Well, and from the sweetness of the flesh, to anoint our mundane lives with the white clay of ecstasy and renew our appetite for life.

The core of this renewal is often a letting-go, or opening-up, a loosening of the boundaries of the self. At best, the world's resistance to our will reminds us to open up a crack in the shell of our identity. It enables us to experience, to behold that which is outside of ourselves—the 'Other'. The Other as people is a familiar other, something we recognize as like ourselves. The material world we behold as much more alien, because it has no human heart. It is this confrontation with the alien otherness of the world outside the self that gives us the opportunity to renew ourselves, to refresh our life-energy, our will to live. When we let go of the shards of will that revolve in the exhausted mind and open up to that unconditioned world, we leave behind the frustration and sadness of our compromises. We find that our perceptions of the world are washed clean by this confrontation, and the doors of our perception are opened to the infinity and eternity of each passing moment.

This opening-up is difficult and demands extraordinary effort. It is often only the major techniques, the big guns of personal change that have the power to catalyze such a shift of viewpoint. Psychedelic sacraments certainly can, and may be the most powerful of such agents, but they have drawbacks in many situations. In my experience the only other technique which consistently approaches that power for change is a form of breathwork.

Breathwork reaches right to the heart of our relationship with the world outside: When we breathe in, we draw a little of that world into our bodies, and we breathe out that which has been part of us. Breathwork techniques have been rediscovered, probably many times, throughout the aeons, so it is hardly surprising that they are ancient enough to have reflections in myth.

THE DEATH OF BREATH AND THE HANGING GOD

I am using the term 'breathwork' to refer to a whole range of practices which have one thing in common: the conscious use of breath to create different states of consciousness. People have probably been using some form of breath technology the world over for tens of thousands of years, but the best documented of the ancient traditions is the Indian science of pranayama. If you google 'pranayama' you will find definitions such as the following:

Pranayama (Sanskrit): from prana ("breath") and yama ("control"). Literally breath control, breath regulation. Pranayama (Sanskrit): from prana, breath + ayama, restraining, stopping.

So: Pranayama is a method of controlling prana or life force through the regulation of breathing.

Nowadays, pranayama tends to have a more specific meaning of the kind of breathwork that you would be trained in by yoga practitioners. Pranayama in this sense is a form of breathwork where each of the four phases of the breath—inhale, hold in, exhale, hold out—is controlled, and the breath is usually held or stopped for increasing lengths of time in the training.

Not all breathwork techniques involve stopping or holding the breath; some emphasize a free movement of breath, a point I will come back to.

Holding the breath whilst the lungs are empty relates to another sense of the word yama, which can also mean death. The Hindu god Yama was the first conscious being ever to die, and so knows all the secrets of death and cessation. He and his sister Yami are the original human twins, a myth-form which recurs across various Indo-European myth cycles, not to mention those of other traditions. One of Yama's titles is Antaka, 'he who ends life'. So, pranayama can be read as 'the death of breath'. The holding of the breath with the lungs empty, also known as *kumbakham*, in the course of breathwork can lead to a still, powerful altered state, what magical writer Pete Carroll has called an 'inhibitory gnosis', which can be used as the basis of magical power or mystical exploration. The power of Yama, to end life, is used to dissolve the stuck sense of self, to break through the hard shell of frustrated will, as a prelude to renewal of the life-force. The feeling of rebirth when the breath stops and starts, when there is finally a rest-point in the breath, followed by the breath spontaneously starting again, has to be experienced to be believed. All the stuff, all the mental processing, that was in the way of ecstatic consciousness just evaporates, and the new breath that then starts is drenched in ecstatic renewal.

Subjectively, this can be an enormously powerful experience. My record here is of an extraordinary breathwork session:

> 'At the end of breath, where it is the same as thought, there lies the emptiness that has the potential of encounter with alien Other. I steer my attention moment to moment by fine-tuning the exact instant and fierceness/softness of breath to maximize a vivid sense of conscious-now. What tells me I am steering in the best direction, is a spectrum of pleasure/discomfort, and sometimes of 'more real/less real'. I am steering along a swerving track of sensation, holding fast to the most 'real' sensation at any given moment. I follow the stretch of a thought in any direction, follow it until the breath dies, ceases to be, and is reborn perfectly in that rightness. I follow it down to strangulation, to the rock-bottom of kumbakham, to the Death of Breath. I pick up every dropped stitch of tension along the way of each single breath. I uproot all the falsity from each breath, all the second-best, ad hoc, it'll-do-ness of each breath. All that is sacrificed to the Death of Breath. As breath dies, it reunites with consciousness. Let the breath remain

> dead until another breath HAS to be taken. At some point, the following breath fuses, becomes coextensive with, thought. The feeling of this pure, renewed breath is like a gesture which I fill with my entire aliveness.
>
> 'The continuity of consciousness is now inescapable, a recognition of the undying awareness that runs underneath the surface of the experience of the death of breath'.

This cessation of normal breath followed by sudden ecstatic re-booting of the breathing sequence is reminiscent of Austin Osman Spare's Death Posture exercise, where the magician overbreathes, restricts the breath, then finally lets go, with the intention of 'wiping' the mind of ordinary thoughts in preparation for magical work. Further, we are reminded of the hanged god, Odin. In Havamal we read:

I know that I hung on a wind-tossed tree
Nights all-nine
Wounded by a spear, given to Odin, myself to myself
On that same tree of which no man knows
From what root it rises
They gave me no bread, nor drinking horn
I looked down
I took up the runes, roaring I took them
And fell back again

Here the god has called upon all that he is not, the Otherness of the mysterious universe, to give him the keys to consciousness, the runes. Although piercing with a spear is mentioned, the sequence starts by referring to hanging, and one of Odin's many titles is Hangatyr, the hanged god, not 'the pierced god'. Clearly, the 'hanging' part of the experience is highly significant. By strangulation, the god cuts off his breath to the point where he stops breathing, where he reaches the edge of death. He has sacrificed himself to himself, confronting his death directly, and been filled with the wisdom of the Other. He surges back from the brink of death, bearing the runes.

TYPES OF BREATHWORK

Most courses of training in yoga, meditation and magic contain basic instruction in pranayama. If you study pranayama at this basic level, you will learn that modulating the flow of breath can be used to temporarily increase physical energy, create relaxation, reduce or increase the intensity of emotion, and clarify the mind to the extent that you become very aware of the stream of your thoughts.

Another effect of breathwork is to increase awareness of bodily energy. Chi Kung and other traditional disciplines which have both martial and healing elements utilize breathing exercises. Some Shamanic-style techniques use overbreathing—intense breathing towards the edge of hyperventilation—which generates a state of highly active emotional and mental arousal that can be used for healing or other magical work. Overbreathing eventually leads to a kind of benign collapse, often into a deep trance state, which may involve 'out of body' experiences.

Connected Breathwork is the technique underlying the Rebirthing and Holotropic breathwork techniques. Rediscovered in the last few decades, it involves simply breathing continuously, without holding the breath and without the stops and pauses which are part of a 'normal' breathing pattern. In connected breathing the breath becomes cyclical. Without beginning or end, the Ourobouros of breath, the Midgard Serpent coiled around the universe, bites its own tail for all eternity. Continual breathing is maintained for up to an hour, or even longer in some circumstances. That is one reason it is called connected breathwork; the other is that it generates a sense of reconnection to suppressed feelings, which in turn results in reconnection to deep sources of inner energy. With a few refinements, this is the basis of a range of extremely powerful techniques for integrating troublesome, uncomfortable and painful emotions and sensations into full-blown bliss. Connected breathwork is often taught with the purpose of bringing the practitioner into ecstasy in present time.

BLISS STATES

You are sitting here, reading this page. How many other activities are going on in your awareness? Take a moment to sit quietly and observe the flow of your thoughts, sensations and feelings. Notice the rhythm of your breath.

Did you find, after a few moments, that you felt like doing something, the beginnings of a desire for some kind of activity? Your active mind may have told you that you are becoming bored, that you need more stimulation. You may want to eat or drink something, to talk to someone, to go out, to read a book, to watch TV, to play on a computer, to pick up the phone and call someone, to get on with some task that needs doing. If you refuse the impulse to act, and instead just sit and do nothing, what happens in your awareness? Again, observe the flow of thoughts, sensations, feelings and desires, and notice the rhythm of your breath.

Did you find, after a few more minutes of stillness, that it was difficult to keep your attention on the rhythm of your breath? That your mind insisted on flooding your attention with thoughts? You may have noticed what some people call the internal monologue—the almost-incessant flow of verbal thoughts, the inner sound of you talking to yourself.

If you have not practiced any form of breathwork before, you may also have noticed that your breath cycle is frequently interrupted—especially when you think!

Now sit quietly again for a few moments, and focus on what is pleasant about your present state. Make up your mind to enjoy the present moment to the utmost.

Did you find, after a few moments, that you got distracted by your thoughts? That stream of thoughts, that internal monologue, is enormously powerful, if it can distract you from enjoying yourself!

Wouldn't it be good if, when you had nothing much to do or think about, you could just go into a bliss state, just feel really good?

And what is stopping you from doing just that? Your little experiment just now suggests that it is the unregulated stream of largely irrelevant and uninteresting thoughts that stands in the way of ecstasy. However, that is just a part of it: in order to feel ecstatic, you have to be in the present moment, really here, now. If you wanted to be somewhere else, or doing something else, you wouldn't be ecstatic now. The only way to feel ecstatic in present time is to be in your body in present time. The boredom of pointless mental activity is a screen which covers our present-time awareness and distracts us from the amazing range of sensations and emotions that flow through us all the time. Connected breathwork teaches us how to let go into the flow of sensation and thereby achieve bliss.

THE CONNECTED BREATHWORK PROCESS AND THE EYE OF THE HAWK

Because you have to be in immediate sensation to experience ecstasy, and because you have no control over the content of the experience, the only material you have to work with—the only kind of experience you have—is the flow of sensations, whatever they are. Some of these feelings and sensations will initially seem uncomfortable, unpleasant or even threatening—but one of the things you will learn in this breathwork is that you can view any sensation you feel in any way you want. Sensations that seemed to be in the way of your achieving ecstasy in the present will be reframed as: interesting; awe-inspiring; full of energy; full of power; beautiful... and, eventually, perfect for this moment. The work you do is: stay relaxed, modulate your breathing as taught, pay attention to the strongest immediate sensation, and change your attitude to that sensation if it seems like it's in the way of your achieving bliss.

Because of this reframing of intense sensations, the process of learning connected breathwork is inevitably a healing journey. You will re-experience blocked or suppressed emotions, maybe as emotions, maybe as energy patterns. As you progressively reframe an unpleasant sensation, feeling it again and again until you start to perceive it as interesting, then positive in some way, a permanent change in the way you relate to that sensation occurs. You may experience this as a kind of 'click'—the sensation has integrated. Integration, in this context, means that a sensation that was once unpleasant will never bother you again; it hasn't gone away, but your attitude to it has changed forever.

This change is permanent because it happens at the level of feeling. It is not necessary to understand where the sensation originally came from, which era of your life, which childhood experience: connected breathwork is not a cognitive technique and is not based on personal history, but on direct sensation and emotion. A sensation may represent unfinished business from earlier today, last week, or 30 years ago, and it doesn't matter. You make no attempt to control which sensations you are experiencing; you work with whatever presents itself to your attention.

The meditational core of this technique is awareness of the present moment, in detail. Your attention is on the intensest sensation you feel, whether it's an itching in your scalp, a numbness in your left thumb, a desire to laugh, an urge to curl up—or something weird like the sense that your right eye is full of pink gas. Your way of perceiving it will be non-judgmental—you cannot but accept this sensation if you are to guide yourself towards feeling ecstatic in present time.

That part of you that perceives without judging, that observes but cannot act, is cultivated by such meditation. You will find yourself becoming more aware of the self-behind-the-self, just watching. It has various names in many traditions and practices. Meditators often call it the 'observing self' or 'choiceless witness'. Austin Osman Spare glyphed it as the Kia, the 'atmospheric I' that sits behind the eyes, that hovers like a vulture above the feast of life and death. We find it too in the Yggdrasil myth that I alluded to at the start of this essay—the Hawk sitting between the eyes of the Eagle atop the tree of life. That Hawk is the ever-present Witness. Further, the falcon or hawk is the beast-vehicle of the goddesses Freya and Frigg in their mode as seeresses. The vision of the entranced priestess is glyphed as the eye of the bird of prey, the eye behind the self, soaring across the vistas of the future to select a prophecy.

EXERCISE

Try Twenty Connected Breaths: This consists of four fairly deep breaths, followed by one really long breath, as deep as you can get it. Repeat this cycle four times, giving you twenty breaths altogether. This brings you into present time in your body. You can do it many times a day. Don't do it whilst driving until you are experienced in feeling the shift in sensation.

SCHOOLS OF BREATHWORK

Rebirthing was discovered (or maybe rediscovered) by a small number of practitioners in the USA in the 1970s. Leonard Orr associated this work with the restimulation of birth trauma memories, and coined the term Rebirthing for his form of connected breathwork. This is a very 'leading' belief, and most clients in Rebirthing sessions will eventually experience birth memories. His students Jim Leonard and Phil Laut reinvented the whole process and called it Vivation. Whilst this may be a clumsy neologism, it does the job of de-coupling connected breathwork from the loaded linguistics of 'rebirthing'. Laut and Leonard emphasized instead the ecstatic features of the experience, rather than programming their students for trauma and 'breakthrough'. As far as they were concerned, what matters is not that people break through traumas, but that they achieve bliss.

In the same period a similar type of breath technology was devised by Stanislav Grof, the brilliant pioneer in the use of psychedelic medicines in psychiatric healing. When his license for entheogens was withdrawn, Grof developed what he called Holotropic Breathwork to be able to get his clients into ecstatic consciousness and do the healing with them.

Other schools of connected breathwork have since been developed. Gay and Kathlyn Hendricks created Radiance Breathwork, and Integrative Breathwork was developed by Jacqueline Small out of holotropic breathwork.

Breaking Convention conference—Solve et Coagula

At last, a British conference on psychedelics! Breaking Convention's first conference in Canterbury in 2011 was a huge success, bringing together different psychedelic narratives—academics, *ayahuasqueros*, counterculture activists young and old, independent researchers and even a chaos magician or three. I gave a talk aimed at putting the magic back into tripping, an account of a successful healing working done on acid.

SOLVE ET COAGULA: PSYCHEDELIC SELF-DISSOLUTION AND SUPERNORMAL ABILITIES BASED ON A TALK GIVEN AT BREAKING CONVENTION 2011

SYNOPSIS:

The psychedelic experience is worthwhile not only for the experiencer's own holotropic (wholeness-seeking) process but also as a powerful key to unlocking healing and other extraordinary abilities. The collapse and reformation of identity typical of entheogen use may be followed by access to healing powers and other unusual abilities.

A relatively rigorous approach to understanding this process may be found in the methodology of Chaos Magic.

INTRODUCTION: PUTTING THE MAGIC BACK INTO THE PSYCHEDELIC EXPERIENCE

One of the most consistent features of the psychedelic experience is a collapse and reformation of the moment-to-moment sense of identity, the continuity of the sense of self that we take for granted. This process may be profoundly healing, and in that case the new identity that is crystallized from molten flux is more useful, more satisfactory, a better self than the old one.

This assembly from chaos of a more effective self has been characterized as holotropic; the word comes from Greek roots meaning 'seeking wholeness'. This is the chief internal aspect of the psychedelic experience.

What is less well studied, particularly in reference to late-industrial (Western) cultures is the use of psychedelic sacraments for access to healing powers and other unusual abilities—the outward-directed face of entheogen use. This kind of practice is familiar from other cultures, such as the ayahuasca shamanism of the Amazon Basin, but is discussed (and probably practised) much less amongst 'Western' psychedelics-using subcultures, even amongst those who identify as magicians.

This article is built round an account of a healing performed in a magical group.

The word 'magic' (sometimes spelt 'magick' to distinguish it from stage conjuring) does need a little more explanation in the modern world. It even feels strange to write the word, writing as I am for an audience outside the magical 'discourse community', the subculture in which people think about and even practise such disciplines as divination and spell-casting.

It seems that, in the wider culture of Western materialism in its Postmodern phase, it is considered OK to practice magic—as long as you are culturally exotic. An Amazon Basin shaman is expected to have beliefs about magic as an integral part of their cultural background, but 'magical thinking' is actually a symptom of insanity in the DSM, the Diagnostic and Statistical Manual of Mental Disorders—the bible of the psychiatric profession. Despite Postmodernism's tolerance of culturally diverse views about the nature of reality, First World culture is dominated by dogmatic scientism, the religion-like adulation of science as the only means of knowing, and if you tell the wrong people about your magical beliefs you risk your reputation for any kind of coherent thought.

There are many definitions of magic. Entire books could be (and have been) written about what magic is. At the deepest level, magical philosophy addresses what the universe is, or how it all works, or what our relationship to it all is. For the purposes of this article, a robust, pragmatic definition will do: Magic(k) is the art and science of causing willed change by means which are poorly understood in terms of physics.

The model of magic I shall be using is Chaos Magic. This is a magical current that began in the late 1970s as a reaction against the psychological interpretations of the ancient mysteries that were prevalent in the 1950s-60s. The previous mainstream magical currents were exemplified by Aleister Crowley's Thelema. To the new generation of magicians, the style of that magic still owed a lot to the current before that, the decidedly Victorian-Masonic format of the Golden Dawn. If we think of 1950s magic as being like over-elaborate Prog Rock, Chaos Magic was the Punk movement that rejected its excesses and showed how little equipment and complex verbiage one needs to obtain magical results. Chaos Magic's mission was to put the practical results back in magic, via a careful analysis of successful magical technique and a rigorous system of training based on the results of that analysis. Its most coherent early exposition is in *Liber Null* by Peter J. Carroll.

Chaos Magic is very helpful to the modern would-be magician, brought up in the anti-magical mainstream, because it's lighter on metaphysics than other magical models. It does not require belief in a spirit world to be effective; in the extreme case that is preferred by some, magical effects can be considered as an exotic species of physics.

THE STORY

Our group tonight numbers thirteen. We are from various magical backgrounds—Chaos Magic, Thelema, Western Tantra. The meeting is at a member's flat in the English Midlands.

There are a number of agendas tonight, one of which is to be a magical working for a group member. For many years she has had an inflamed bowel, and it has recently got much worse.

For the healing, one participant is to do a kind of psychic surgery, extracting the magical form of the disease and neutralizing it.

A broadside of consciousness-raising techniques are used over a few hours. First, there's a warm-up which includes listening to the William Burroughs sound piece 'Apocalypse', and doing some shaking to get a sense of energy moving through the body. Those who wish to, including the member who is to be the healer, also take a psychedelic sacrament. A banishing ritual is performed, to mark the departure from normal life into magical consciousness. To complete the opening stages, a priest is chosen. He is to have the 'Beast-God/Goddess' Baphomet[25] invoked into him, so that he speaks as the God/dess.

The evening's work is to be spread out over about four hours, leading up to the climactic healing working.

When the time comes, the healer crouches over the recipient, breathing convulsively. It looks like he knows what to do: with a small, sharp blade he cuts the side of his hand, then dips his finger in the blood and draws a triangle on the patient's belly. Then it seems like he is wrestling with the triangle; it represents the disease, and he has to remove it by lifting each corner, loosening it, until it is free and can be lifted clear of the patient.

He is struggling with the pattern, going into a kind of mad overbreathing, shouting and hissing and tearing at the miasm corner by corner until, quite suddenly, he slumps back and uncurls himself so that he is lying down, relaxing at last. The pattern has been torn out.

Is the patient healed? A couple of hours later, long after the workings had finished, she has a rather scary crisis. Walking across the room, she suddenly keels over, fainting. We rally round and feed energy to her. She recovers rapidly.

According to her own reports, the condition never recurred. Weeks, months, years later, and it remains healed.

So what was going on there?

The patient got healed; the healer felt her flesh as something very different to how flesh usually feels, with far fewer limitations as to what can be done with it. Suddenly, it was possible to intervene in the structure of someone else's flesh in ways that he wouldn't normally consider possible.

How can we model this effect, so as to understand and maybe reproduce it?

---

[25] This is Baphomet in the sense used by Chaos Magicians. One guide to this interpretation of Baphomet is Peter Carroll's 'Notes on Baphomet', which can be read online at https://mandrakespeaks.wordpress.com/essays/notes-on-baphomet-peter-carroll/; for an in-depth study of the magical dimensions of this form, see *The Book of Baphomet* by Nikki Wyrd and Julian Vayne.

THE MODEL

Let us examine what happened there in the most general terms, using a Chaos Magic model.

In a nutshell, the core theory of Chaos Magic is that two things are important in magical action: Belief and Gnosis. The latter is what is more commonly called an altered state of consciousness or ASC. I prefer the term extraordinary state of consciousness or ESC.

The core of magic is the shift in belief. The most basic belief shift necessary, that underlies all the others, is that magic is possible. As I mentioned above, this runs counter to most of our conditioning in modern cultures, and so requires a good deal of work for most people. Within that envelope, we each have to believe that we are magicians. This is harder still, and comes only gradually, through repeated exposure to magical events. I have witnessed numerous miracles (I write about the most impressive of them in *Bright From the Well*), so I have become more comfortable with those two nested beliefs.

Within that daily belief in the magical nature of their life, the magician then has to choose the specific outcome he or she wants. Now comes the technical stage; there are an infinite number of ways to do the next bit, and the choice of method will depend on personal factors. Popular examples of how this next stage is done could be to symbolize the outcome in some way, or to conceal it in a sigil (a visual device) or mantra (a sound pattern). Whatever method they use to create it, this is the magical device they will use for the next stage.

The other main factor, gnosis or ESC, is used to loosen up the mind's activity so that the magical device can be focused on and allowed to enter the deeper layers of the magician's mind. If it all works well, that pattern then does its inscrutable work in the unconscious layers of the magician's psyche. Another way of looking at a successful result is that we flow, or pour ourselves, into a new reality, one of which includes the change we intended.

The techniques of gnosis include arousal, such as dancing, singing or sex, as well as quiescent methods such as sitting meditation. The objective in both cases is that belief becomes fluid, and we allow ourselves to enter the new reality we have willed.

With psychedelic workings, there is always enough gnosis—reality is quite fluid enough. Let us look more closely at the dissolution phase of the experience, and one property of that phase we are particularly interested in: plasticity.

Psychedelics dissolve boundaries within us. It seems that the resultant molten chaos can be entrained into useful new forms, useful new realities, into willed purposes. James Kent, in his recent book *Psychedelic Information Theory*, dissects this process:

> *'... even though psychedelics destabilize top-down control of consciousness, feedback control and linear system stability can be entrained back into coherence via external periodic drivers, including rhythmic motor activity, drumming, singing, chanting, rocking back and forth, dancing, and so on. It is no accident that these are also the basic formal elements of shamanic ritual.'*

The techniques Kent mentions are examples of what I went into above—the particular techniques the magician (or shaman) uses to encode their desired outcome. In the context of a psychedelic ritual, these techniques provide a structuring, patterning influence which entrains the billowing chaos of moment-to-moment experience.

THE INTENSITY OF THE STATE AND THE WEIRDNESS OF THE MAGIC

In this section, I examine the relationship between how magical an event is, and how extreme the state that seemed to lead to it was. The basic idea is that the more magical an event is, the more extraordinary must be the state of consciousness that caused it.[26]

A SCALE OF WEIRDNESS

What makes a result magical? I would say: the degree of apparent improbability of the result. In other words, the weirder an event is (allowing for context), the more magical. In my decades of magical work, I have witnessed and experienced many apparently 'miraculous' events. Those that seem to be down to magical work I have categorized into five levels, making up a qualitative scale for the degree of improbability of an event intruding into reality—a scale for the degree of weirdness of an event. A full account of the model and the anecdotes which support it are in my book *Bright From the Well.*

Level 1: I call this Body Alchemy. These effects are apparently caused by the action of will entirely within the skin, or involving recordable, non-occult communication between skin-bounded humans.

This is what psychologists might call a holistic-psychological effect. There is actually nothing here to challenge materialistic scientism. The will acts via some subconscious instruction to change gene expression. This type of causality includes firewalking, wart-charming, most forms of healing and the so-called placebo effect, which is, of course, healing magic. At the

---

[26] In fact, it is never possible to be certain of a causal link between a magical action and a desired (or disastrous) result. Some despair and attempt to eschew causality. I recommend meditating on this paradox by asking yourself: Why do I practice magic?

Another warning on this issue: some magicians, those on the mystical side, would question any notion of causality in magic on a philosophical basis. Jung's definition of synchronicity as an 'acausal connecting principle' is of a piece with this line of thinking.

extreme end of Body Alchemy there exist effects such as setting fire to things by gazing at them.

Visions, virtual encounters with other realities, have a similar or lower level of weirdness, unless they contain checkable data that couldn't have been arrived at any other way; that raises the weirdness to Level 3 or 4.

Despite the impressiveness of some of the effects, it could be said that Level 1/Body Alchemy isn't really magic at all, because science can, with an increasingly small stretch, explain it. For example, the finding that immune system cells communicate with central nervous system sites was one of the discoveries that narrowed the gap and enabled more materialistic scientists to take the plunge of believing in psychosomatic healing.

Level 2 events show effects which are not confined to the skin. I label this level of abilities Transpersonal, meaning that instructions and other information appear to be transferred between two or more people's nervous systems without the usual means. The magics of this level include telepathy, the unconscious transmission of information in situations such as one person's psychic state being picked up by another, and any magical result where information seems to have been transferred by unknown means.

With *Level 3* we seem to be looking at something which not only suggests communication between nervous systems, but some kind of coordination of effects between more than two nervous systems. One of the most vivid examples of this kind of magic was when a friend of mine obtained the phone number of a friend who was long out of touch, from the numbers in a tarot spread.

One of the definitions of magic I like is Pete Carroll's: the engineering of synchronicities. I'd label this level as Strong Transpersonal and also as Synchronistic. With such results, it seems as if the world is a matrix, or an operating system, or a field of interconnected consciousnesses.

Some experiences take us even beyond this, where the non-human world itself seems to be affected directly by our magic. *Level 4* consists of strong Synchronistic events, effects that seem to be only partially dependent on a human brain receiving the information put out there. Once, to test a new magical working, I and three others appeared to interfere with the sound on the BBC Nine O'Clock News.

This is what is popularly thought-of as being magic, in the Harry Potter sense: events with no apparent physical connection bend the rules of probability; effects occur as if will acts directly on the physical universe, without the intermediary of a human receiver. Specific abilities at this level include remote viewing, as well as any improbable, 'inexplicable' result in consensus reality that *appears* to be a result of your magical action.

Finally, for *Level 5,* we have events that seem to demonstrate direct effects on matter, like forces applied to objects. Effects at this level include psychokinesis—objects flying across the room, people levitating—and the random leakage of this sort of energy that leads to poltergeist activity.

THE INTENSITY OF THE STATE

Compared to classifying strange events, it is much harder to draw up a scale for 'extraordinariness' of one's state of consciousness, what we could call 'degree of gnosis', because of the unreliability of subjective measures of magical ability. However, three levels of psychedelic-magical ESC (Extraordinary State of Consciousness), and the levels of magical effect they might link to, are suggested:

ESC 1: A stage where the flesh seems 'molten' or plastic. This is relatively easy to identify, and corresponds with effects like those in the above anecdote, which was a tale of radical body alchemy.

ESC 2: A sense of minds overlapping; this is the level at which it seems that telepathy can happen.

ESC 3: A state in which the very reality around you seems molten or plastic. It may seem as though you are directly apprehending a menu of probabilities, in which various 'shadow' versions of the future may or may not exist. This subjective level would correspond to effects at weirdness level 4.

I do not propose a specific ESC corresponding to the power to create Level 5 events because they vary so much in degree of weirdness. Also, they are hard to understand even when we invoke shadow-futures. Smaller scale energy effects, like causing paper to burst into flames by directing energy at it, are almost certainly generated by control of microwave emissions from the body, so fall into the extreme end of the Level 1 spectrum, Body Alchemy.

The larger-scale psychokinetic effects are inexplicable in terms of any conventional current notions of the transformation of physical energy. They are also so rare, even for people with their eyes open to spot them and with their prejudices against witnessing exceptional events turned off (magicians), that it's hard even to narrow down the conditions under which they occur.

CONCLUDING REMARKS

Magic, the forgotten mother of Western culture, can be awoken and brought back into play by believing in it, as long as our approach is rigorous enough. I believe the Chaos Magic model to be sufficiently rigorous and to form the most effective bridge yet built between magic and the modern world. The kind of frameworks outlined above are useful starting points for non-religious, pragmatic magical understandings of psychedelic trances.

Of course, psychedelic gnosis is not for everyone. And that goes double for psychedelic magic. It is definitely not something that should be attempted without years of magical and psychedelic training. The psychedelic state needs to be thoroughly explored, so that the psychonaut has plenty of experience in hauling themselves out of dark corners and repairing any energy leaks that may occur. Magical training needs to be pursued to the point where concentration and mental steadiness is far above the level that most people find adequate. This generates a kind of mental steadiness both during and after the psychedelic voyage. The third necessity for doing magic on psychedelics is to be a member of a genuine, traditional shamanic lineage or alternatively a very strong, magically experienced community that can act to ground the trainee and situate his or her experiences in a constructive narrative.

To round this piece off, it does need to be said that the above ideas are basically modern versions of processes and experiences that are dealt with in ancient tales and myths. The apparent paradox of the pairing of the surrender of the sense of self and subsequent empowerment can be seen as two phases of a cycle. We see this view emerge in traditional accounts of magical transformation.

In the Old Norse poem *Havamal*,[27] we read:

> *I know that I hung, on a wind-swept tree*
> *for all of nine nights,*
> *wounded by spear, and given to Odin*
> *myself to myself,*
> *on that tree of which no man knows*
> *from what root it rises.*
> *They dealt me no bread, nor drinking horn*
> *I looked down, I drew up the runes,*
> *screaming I took them up,*
> *and fell back from there.*
> ……
> *Then I began to grow*
> *and waxed well in wisdom.*
> *One word led me to another,*
> *one work led me to another.*

One reading we can make of these verses is: The mind is suspended in a billowing flux—the windy tree; the sacrifice of known-self to emergent Self is an ordeal in which we uncover the mysteries, that lie beneath the

[27] James Allen Chisholm, *The Eddas, Keys to the Mysteries of the North*, Stanzas 138–141.

surface (down); we draw those new patterns out of chaos and into consciousness; we fall back into the mundane and, in so doing, we gather magical power with which to change the world we live in.

Seek the Mysteries!

What is Tripping For?

The following piece was originally intended as a blog post. I then decided it would work better here. I'm asking much the same question as I did in the article that opens Part 2, but from a number of years later.

WHAT IS TRIPPING FOR?

What do people use psychedelics for? When I first took acid in 1969 some of my co-trippers represented the tail-end of a subculture whose main answer to that question was: *instant enlightenment.* This aspiration was enshrined in Country Joe's beautiful song 'Bass Strings' with its refrain that referred to the belief that the next dose of acid would lead to a permanent high. Among the memoirs of that time, William Craddock's *Be Not Content* stands out for its writing quality, and is a typical story of someone who sets out to do just that, using acid to break through into enlightenment without all the tedium of actual consistent practice. In the course of that quest, he and his friends pretty much destroy themselves; some of the people on the tripping scene I came into at age 18 were heading that way.

That subcultural meme derived at least in part from Timothy Leary's *The Psychedelic Experience*, a tripping manual which used the *Tibetan Book of the Dead*'s bardo stages as a model for a guided, high-dose trip. As a result of the subcultural dominance of this text, a lot of people came to confuse the two things and believe that all you had to do was read the book, drop 500 mics and hunker down into the White Light of the Void. In other words, the map got conflated with the territory. I was in a sense a junior member of a cohort that had volunteered to test that 'instant enlightenment' hypothesis. But it was a while before it became abundantly clear that only a small percentage of people who took a lot of acid got spiritually awakened in any meaningful, long-term sense.

Make no mistake—you can get the experience. I had the cosmic consciousness trip, me and the entire cosmos dissolving completely then reforming. But there's a big difference between an experience, or a *state* of consciousness, and a *stage* of inner development. In other words, that utterly cosmic experience was a teaser, no more. No one around me meditated, or did any regular magical work, any discipline that might ground and integrate the blasting light of Eternity. I don't think anyone around me had even heard of magic. In fact, it's probably fair to say that some of my friends would have looked down on anyone who did apply themselves consistently to their inner development. Well, maybe not looked down on, more looked askance at, with a certain grudging respect for anyone who would scale the Sacred Mountain on foot rather than just keep taking the LSD helicopter in the hope that one day they'd be able to live up there on the mountain-top.[28]

[28] I develop this metaphor for tripping and spiritual awakening in a talk titled 'DaveLee SacredMountain+LSD helicopter' which can be found on the Chaotopia YouTube channel. Apologies for the poor sound quality.

So I didn't know what to do with that searing glimpse of the void. I did acid loads more times, often setting up what my friend Bug called 'wipeout trips'. This amounted to an attempt to recover or attain the ground of being, by dint of lying around listening to music on high doses. A variation on this practice was to lie around in a natural setting. I found I couldn't replicate the cosmic experience, or anything like it, with further doses of acid. That massive teaser had pointed to a stage that, if I could continue believing in it, was surely decades of daily work ahead. So I did what my friends did, trying other drugs, any drugs that might give me a field of experience in which I could maybe evaluate what had happened to me when the Eye of Shiva opened and the universe dissolved.

I had two years of this lifestyle, then decided it was going nowhere. That isn't to say I didn't have a lot of vitally important experiences, some of which led me eventually into consistent magical practice, but the instant enlightenment thing was a bust. The whole idea started to look like the result of a misperception, a confusion of the menu with the meal; on a bad day, it looked like a hype. In any event, the experiment had failed. I got myself a new life, as a science student. Then, a few years later, I started studying magic properly, and actually doing some work.

But there was always a seemingly unbridgeable gulf between my new magical practice—the daily concentrations and meditations, the dreamwork, the spells, sigils, mantras and pathworkings—and those memories of vast psychedelic perspectives. There were no usable psychedelic-magical maps, once I'd stepped out of the mystical attainment frame. The experimental, multi-model chaos magic approach was the beginning of my making sense of all that.

But it took a few years. Ritual magic is at the other end of a vast spectrum of consciousness from high-dose tripping. That degree of moltenness just doesn't work well with scripts and ritual gestures. However, the early magical groups I was involved with developed ways of using relatively low dosages combined with other ritual techniques. We experimented rather widely, and eventually created something quite ambitious—a group mind or egregore entity (more of which in Part 4 of this book), which was an astonishing focus of magical effectiveness for years. Group ritual became another way to use psychedelics; as long as you stuck to fairly low doses.

In my early 40s I plunged into the healing and integration side of inner work. I qualified in connected breathwork and started experimenting with high-dose psychedelics again. The objectives then were a combination of emotional healing and transpersonal ecstasy. A friend and I took turns to sit for each other on high doses combined with connected breathwork. This was my third main use for psychedelics.

This kind of work is of course coming right into the mainstream of psychotherapy and psychiatry. For reminiscences from the earliest generation of psychedelic psychotherapist check out this recent one-hour podcast with Stanislav Grof, who was tripping and healing back in the 1950s, and Brigitte Grof.

The marketing at the start of that podcast refers to legal access to psychedelic healing experiences in some centre somewhere. That reminds me of a recent series called *Nine Perfect Strangers.*[29]

When I first noticed this I really didn't think it would be my kind of thing. But friends advised me otherwise, and I'd agree—watch it. It's about psychedelic psychotherapy, and asks some very interesting questions; no spoilers, it's a good drama!

Here is a thoughtful piece from an experienced psychedelic guide/ sitter, Rosalind Watts of the UCL team.[30]

Psychedelic medicine is sufficiently mainstream now that even respectable academia—Johns Hopkins university for instance—wants data from people who have been doing this illegally for decades. From us freaks, in other words.

Healing is a great use for these amazing medicines. But how does their medicalization affect (or afflict) our experience of using them? Will they become 'tamed', our mental set around them so changed that they no longer offer the limitless chaos that promises total transformation? In other words, do we need to overcome the medicalization of psychedelic substances?

Maybe we have to go much deeper and higher than we think, if we want to heal; we cannot afford to sideline ecstasy and 'mystical' experience. In so doing, we may find that we've thrown out the bathwater of religion with the baby of an important conceptual framework for our tripping. In a superb article Alexander Beiner asks:

> *But what if your culture can't help you contextualise your experience, because it doesn't have space for the sacred and transcendent? Here lies the problem of psychedelic capitalism.*[31]

Beiner suggests that psychedelic medicine is a Trojan horse, a cunning way of making these substances respectable enough to reintroduce them into mainstream society. This won't happen of its own accord—it is up to us to build a narrative about psychedelics that can reach into the mainstream.

---

[29] 2021, *Nine Perfect Strangers.*

[30] Watts R. (2022, February 28th). 'Can magic mushrooms unlock depression? What I've learned in the five years since my TEDx talk', Medium.

[31] Beiner A. (2021). 'The Psychedelic Trojan Horse', The Bigger Picture.

What models of tripping have we got and how useful might they be as elements of such a narrative?

First off, it's more than therapy. The therapy model doesn't always fit; you lie down, put on your eyeshades and headphones, cue up your playlist, and... not much happens. Or some emotional healing occurs, and then it ends and you know that nothing more in that direction is going to happen on this occasion, so eventually you get up and do something else.

It's also more than meditation. The kind of experience where you cultivate stillness and equanimity while the world warps and shatters around you does fit some parts of some trips. But I think that description of meditation applies more to the basic attitude of the tripper than it does to the purpose of the session.

It's not practical magic, an activity designed to have an effect on the world in the form of well-defined outcomes linked to magical symbols. However, it does sometimes feel as though the deep effects we feel within ourselves are there because we care, because we have staked so much on our caring, which is leading us into a deeper transformation and in so doing has subtle but important effects on the world.

This process might include some vision of the world as forever being damaged, and our experience of witnessing that damage as being in some mysterious way healing for it.

Sometimes people think of a trip as an underworld journey. We enter the depths and our normal selfhood falls apart. The entry into the underworld sometimes feels like a rehearsal for dying. We may even meet the cosmic other, the Fetch, the Valkyrie, as a radiant psychedelic lover, who will come once more for us trailing clouds of fire and beauty and terror when we begin the process of our own death. At the end of the underworld experience, we are reassembled and emerge into the dayside again, with a new vision, something that renews us, and that we can share with our fellows.

This underworld journey can take the form of a process of witnessing and articulating to ourselves thoughts and feelings at the edge of selfhood. We are in a shadow zone where we aren't anything like what we usually think of ourselves as, but we feel that we simply have to process the racing chaos of impressions in real time. That mental activity is a constant iteration of a search for coherence in a state of incoherence.

The function of that activity is to see the world in a radically different way, so different that it's an inversion of our usual reality. The paradox is that the reality of the underworld is a truer reality.

That reorientation to a radically different truth is at the core of the process. Beiner (same article) writes:

> *The sacred is not there to make our lives better. It is not there to confirm our warped ideologies. It is there to shred us. It guides us to the depths of ourselves*

> *to find our own delusions and dispel them.*
> *This aspect of the sacred—its capacity to reveal the deep pathology of the cultural games we play—is the burning heart of the psychedelic counterculture. Without honouring it, psychedelics won't transform culture. They won't help us to address the problems we've created for ourselves, whether mental illness or ecological collapse.*
> *They can only do that if we allow them to reveal our own cultural madness until it's so undeniable we have no choice but to transform.*

This could be the central cultural reason for using psychedelics, a process of underworld journeying. A deep gnosis that is perpetually renewed, so that the whole culture might be re-birthed, again and again, a sharing of what we bring back from our journeys to contribute to a collective cultural dream space. This ongoing process has no end in sight, it's a project that will span generations, an ongoing initiation at the core of society.

Part 3: Landscape and the Runes

The categories of magic connect up and overlap; psychedelic gnosis often works best in connection with landscape, and can open up into immersion in some epiphany of place and immediate presence, maybe even an embodied sense of the infinite. From my earliest magical studies, earth mysteries and psychogeography promised new and vivid inner experiences.

In turn, earth mysteries and psychedelic gnosis connect us to what our culture has half-forgotten, to the layers of history laid down in our landscapes and in the names and characters of our towns, and beyond that, to the traces of ancient myths that connect to particular places.

I moved to Sheffield in 1967, when I was 16. My parents were rejoining a Northern branch of our family, leaving the suburbs of London for a town I barely knew. Subsequently I left Sheffield to live in a number of other towns, and increasingly, I got interested in the history and folklore of every place I lived. When I moved back to Sheffield in 2003, I walked all over, and started to read about the places I was seeing.

'Sheffield' is a modern version of the Saxon 'Escafeld', which means 'border clearing'. Escafeld was a border town between the mediaeval kingdoms of Mercia and Northumbria, before England was united into a single nation. This geographical liminality is reprised in various other local place names: I live in an area called Meersbrook, and in another Saxon dialect, this translates as 'boundary-brook'. Much of the Meersbrook is now culverted up to where it joins another boundary river, the Sheaf. This is what is left of the border between Sheffield and Derbyshire, which in turn used to be the boundary between Mercia and Northumberland.

In the Noughties I belonged to the chaos magic group WASUME, who also occasionally did public performances of rune-galdor. We used a stylized image of Sheffield's rivers and streams as a sigil. At the start of the group, we took a map of Sheffield and randomly marked it eight times. We picked somewhere close to each site—a bus route over the ring road, a casino, a view of a sewage farm, a hill from where we could see the stars—and did magical workings suggested by the site itself. This had the effect of binding the group to the area we were working in and, as a side effect, quietly inventing Randonauting before it bore that name.

A few years later a magical friend introduced me to *The Hall of Waltheof*, by Sidney Oldall Addy. This is an 1893 book about the origins of the place names in Sheffield, with particular emphasis on the hall of Saxon Earl Waltheof mentioned in *Domesday Book*. Waltheof opposed William the Bastard's brutal occupation and paid the price; no-one is quite sure where his hall, which gave rise to the local place name Hallam, actually stood. Oddy's archaeological and linguistic forays may not be rigorous by the standards of modern academic history, but they painted a poetic picture of old Sheffield that gave me whole new layers of magical significance.

Inspired in part by *The Hall of Waltheof*, I went out on some walks around my town, in interesting states of consciousness. What the French Situationist radical artists of the 1950s called *dérives*, drifts. The experiences were ways of exploring history, of the place as written and of the place as I remember it, but the overall intention was to drift aimlessly, and to be open to the *feel* of where I walked, to the magical edges of the everyday things around me.

Here are some excerpts from my diary:

I walk from the centre of town up West Street to Weston Park. It occurs to me to go through the University grounds, then into the Students' Union, for the first time in many years. It's all changed—the bridge to the entrance is gone, is part of the inside of the building. Outside becomes inside. Downstairs, where the bar is and was, memories flood back—I lived in this area in 1971 and frequented that bar. The social scene I was on floated on a small ocean of LSD. Then I found myself in exactly the spot where I had a time-warp experience in May 1971, a version of myself that lived in eternity gave me a message that is still working itself out. So I complete a circuit in time.

*

In Weston Park Museum: The burial urn mentioned in *The Hall of Waltheof* is not instantly impressive in appearance, but then I notice the pattern cut into it, similar entoptic grids to those on the drinking vessels of the 'Beaker People', the sheep-herders who, some anthropologists say, drank psychedelic sacraments from such vessels.

*

I walk down Broomspring Lane, remembering the places I lived round here in 1970–71. I walk past the end of Holberry Place, which used to be called Havelock Square at that time. Ironical, in light of the attempted upmarket rebranding of the area, renaming the street after a local Chartist hero, that it was the site of Sheffield's very own anarchist commune in the years 1970–73.

*

I go up to the top of Crookes, in time for sunset. The dry, bright cold we call bracing. I take a bus and as soon as I get off, I'm looking at a memorial plaque. It's all about death today.

I walk up the hill. Smells of fried fish, laughing people, the atmosphere of a market. I go up Bole Hill Lane, Tinker Lane, to the Bole Hills park. The sunset is pink and takes up two thirds of the sky. The view is stunning, I got here just in time.

Whether or not Waltheof had his hall here, I bet someone did. A good place to defend your home from—it must be the biggest view in the Sheffield urban area. A good place to live, and a dramatic place to die.

Water is turning into slush underfoot, it's getting really cold. Death is indeed the theme. Not surprising, in view of recent bereavements. As if to underline that pattern, a police helicopter dips over, beating chilly winds of apocalypse.

I walk down through Walkley, then Upperthorpe, where a long-dead friend once lived. I salute the memory of a man who taught me that dead ideas make a fine bonfire.

The more I got into the Waltheof material, the deeper it went. Reading to the end of the book, I found this note appended after the main text:

> *The old Northern poem called the Lay of Righ ... attributed to the eleventh century, describes the characteristics of the three orders of men, viz., thralls,*

> *yeomen, and gentlemen. The Earl, according to the poem, lived in a hall facing the south. He began to be a warrior, and:*
> *"He began to waken war, he began to redden the field, he began to fell the doomed; he won himself lands. He ruled alone over eighteen townships".*
> *Messrs. Vigfusson and Powell, the editors of the poem, say that it is "clearly of Western origin", in other words that it originated in the British Isles. Now Waltheof, or Val-þjófr (put to death in 1075), was the acknowledged chief and leader of Danish or Northern England.*
> *According to the Doomsday Book he not only had a hall in Hallamshire, but "ruled alone over eighteen townships" there. These were the townships of Sheffield and Attercliffe, which were "inland" of the manor of Hallam, and the sixteen unnamed berewicks, mentioned in the Survey.*
> *In the second line, and perhaps in the alliteration, the poet seems to be punning on the word val in Val-þjófr. Can we not, therefore, say that the lay was sung at Waltheof's court, and was intended to flatter or please him? It belongs to the class of genealogical poems. It contains a description of an Earl's house, and of the food, clothing, personal appearance, etc., of its noble inmates.*

When I started studying the Icelandic poems known as the *Eddas* in the late 1990s, I was drawn to the *Rigsthula*, the *List of Rig*. It was the first Eddic tale I played around with to make a story of my own, 'Rig's Tale'. This story became the first part of my 'Master Work of Lore' for the Rune-Gild, the book that was eventually published as *Bright From the Well*.[32] The notion that the *Rigsthula* may have been sung in Waltheof's hall, or even written for him or his father Siward may—or may not—be true, but I choose to believe it for poetic reasons.

An earlier walk connected me to the landscape and the story of my biological family. I was adopted as a baby, so I have no conscious memory of my blood-family. Eventually, via a series of extraordinary 'coincidences', and during my preparation for a pilgrimage, I found them. I shall tell this story in more detail in a later memoir.

It was summer 1995, and my pilgrimage consisted of walking over 40 miles to Avebury, along the ancient track known as the Ridgeway, and then invoking my Holy Guardian Angel. I'd been preparing for this for some time of course, using the Bornless One ritual in various forms and working with a Goetia group in the Midlands.

It was a success, of a weird sort. The vision came, a glimpse of eternity refracted through images I knew were already past being any further use. The vision supplied a new perspective, but it was a finger pointing in a new direction, towards a new adventure I had to go on straightaway. This one

---

[32] Lee D. (2008). *Bright From the Well*, Mandrake of Oxford.

started with a visit to South London to see the founder of the Rune-Gild, Edred Thorsson, speak for the first time in the UK.

I parked outside the venue, barely in time, so I didn't bother to clear visible items off the car seats. The talk was an inspiring exposition of a Northern magic path that answered some of the questions I'd been asking about my direction. I can still remember some vivid moments, which is more than I can about most talks I've been to. I was in an intensely receptive state after my recent magical experiences, and this was obviously the new current of work I was being pointed towards.

When the talk had ended and I got back outside, the car's little side window was broken, and my bag gone. Mostly, it contained a black robe, a wand, and a Solomonic pentacle on parchment; in short, all the thief got was my kit for doing Goetia, plus a change of underwear. I hope it illuminated them; their theft underlined the fact that one phase of my magical life was at an end and a new one was beginning. A few months later, in January 1996 I joined the Rune-Gild.

The mysteries of place and history are a big part of what attracted me to the study and practice of the so-called Northern Mysteries: the runes, and the old gods of North-West Europe. The *dérives* I described above were successful attempts to connect with a feeling, which I tentatively called 'depth', though *balance* might be nearer the mark. The paradigm-hopping that chaos magic is famous (or notorious) for is good magic and vitally important mental hygiene for anyone who has entered into the liminal spaces of Chapel Perilous. But it can lazily default to Scientism as the main thing, a reflex sidelining of the weirder ontological implications of ecstatic states. The Sword of Reason needs to be balanced with the Wand of Intuition, not to mention the perspectives provided by the Lamp of Illumination, which may shine with the light of the non-dual or with the darkness of primal chaos, the unnameable dimensions of embodied ecstasy. I needed to find the magic in the history of my own culture, in the layers before Christianity.

As chaos magicians, we spend a lot of mental effort getting into different contrasting and even mutually exclusive belief systems, mind-sets, reality tunnels. We live next to a revolving door between Scientism and Magic. What might it feel like to get into the mind set of pre-Christian ancestors? Not for just one ritual, but as a project of embedding myself in that current again and again?

And so, I joined another magical organization. What *attracts* us to an organization is what it appears to be about, but what prompts us to *actually join it* is the people involved. I met Ian Read and Ingrid Fischer when they were running the first London group of the IOT. Not long after, when Pete Carroll retired from active participation, they ran the UK Section of the organization. As I got to know them, I understood the depth of their interest in the Northern current of magic.

The magic of the Northern current is present in a number of poems and stories such as the *Eddas,* and is visible in the saga literature. Much more of that mythic culture is half-hidden, half-visible in ancient art and odd forgotten corners of culture. The well is obscured, but it's still there. And many people have drawn from it, for good or ill. It probably won't have escaped your notice that the runes and Northern magic have a tarnished reputation in some quarters. We still have some way to go in clearing up misconceptions about Germanic esotericism *per se* by telling the actual history of how the Nazis cherry-picked bits of Germanic tradition to dramatize and glamourize the banality of their murderous politics. In my book *Bright From The Well* I celebrate a vision of an untainted well: a source that is not in itself polluted, just because some criminally insane elements took water from it to brew poison.

There are still a few contemporary Germanic esotericists who insist that Germanic esoteric work should have a political dimension. This is what, using Northern terminology, I would call the *thursic* side of the tradition. *Thurses* are the dumb, destructive giants in the old Northern tales and they provide, as mythic truths often do, useful tools for thinking about the modern world. *Thurses* are characterized by stupidity. Everything about them stinks of automatism and unconsciousness. They represent the undertow of human consciousness, the forces of habituated, ignorant resistance that lurk beneath the conscious will. Anything dumb, infantile and socially destructive can be seen as a *thurs*. Racism is a good example; it can be framed as the reification of imperialistic ideas using the most primitive elements of human consciousness, the elements that reduce us to the subhuman. Racists are people on a deep dive into the world of the Untermensch.

The essay below, 'Three Thurses For Thee', outlines a model of some of the destructive forces in society using this kind of idea. It was presented as a talk at the Rune-Gild World Moot in 2011. It's the first time I had Scientism in my sights. It's a bit of a rant.

THREE THURSES FOR THEE: TOWARDS A DEMONOLOGY OF CONSUMERISM

Consider this pair of familiar propositions:

- We are all in a dream most of the time.
- We can choose to wake up, but it takes work, and this is the Work of initiation.

So, in what sense are we in a dream?

Imagine you are watching TV, and you see an advert featuring sizzling rashers of bacon. Your mouth waters. You get up and go into the kitchen. You catch yourself, frying pan in hand, at the point you realise you aren't actually hungry. No harm done.

Now imagine you are riding in a car along a city street. You are wide awake, as aware as it gets. From a billboard, you see a face smiling down at you, lips parted, eyes moist and luminous... this is not just a rumbling in your stomach that emulates hunger, this is real desire; lust and happiness are fused in the eyes of the beloved, the woman, man, or beast of your dreams that is used in that car or coffee or toothpaste advert. That image has wormed its way into your inner world, and it will keep on generating feelings. If they're pleasant feelings, you will probably not resist its internalization. It has become part of you, a powerful element in your mythic world.

We are all in a dream of this kind; that's what the mystics have been telling us for thousands of years: from Lao-Tse through to Plato.

We are all in a dream; that's what critics of consumerism tell us too. In the words of Walter Benjamin, 'the advertisement is one method whereby the commodity infiltrates the dream-world of the consumer'.

In critiquing consumerism, we may come to understand some important lessons for our illumination.

In doing so, we are following an ancient initiatory process. By unmasking and learning how to resist these thurses, we come to free ourselves from their grip, and so we become more conscious.

So what are these forces, and to what extent are they thursic?

I expect many of you will have heard of Crowley's Aeonics, that succession of principles around which human spirituality organizes itself in each historical era.

First there is Isis the Mother, the Pagan Aeon, ruled by the laws of Nature; then Osiris the Father, the Aeon of monotheism and most recently (1904 according to Crowley) Horus, the Crowned and Conquering Child, the beginning of the maturation of humanity beyond repressive laws.

Before I'd even heard of magick, I was a natural child of the Horus aeon. Freedom was my game. Richard Neville's *Playpower*, a famous (and famously overrated) book from the years of my youth, gave us a term that seemed to make sense.

And some of the things I dreamed about in the Playpower phase of my youth have come true, and I hate them.

As a youngster in the early 1970s, viewing the ruined industrial landscapes of North-East Sheffield's Attercliffe and Tinsley, the bit you see when you pass between turnoffs 32 and 31 of the M1 motorway, I remember thinking that they should be replaced by a children's playground.

That dream came true, in a warped way: the monstrous Meadowhall mall sprouted on the site of the steel industries' ruin. I served my time there in the run-up to Yule 1995, the Xmas feeding frenzy, running a stall selling my aromatics company's products. Every day, driving home, I played the most nihilistic industrial rock I could find, to try and banish that consumerist hell.

But the Aeon of Horus was needed: much of the old world had to go—in particular, the insane sexual repression of the Victorian era, which was dealt a significant blow by the lifestyle rebellion of the Sixties. The Aeon of Horus was still making sense.

It still made sense to me in 1997, when I wrote *Chaotopia!*. In that book, I prized neoteny, which, biologically speaking is when individuals reach sexual maturity without developing all the other adult characteristics of their species. Neoteny is therefore a metaphor for continual openness to development.

That open-endedness is the crown and the burden of humankind—that we are creatures of chaos, that we don't really know what we are. That means we can and do become anything—our freedom produces Auschwitz, and Beethoven, James Joyce and Big Brother. So I stand by my defence of neoteny—minds that are flexible and adaptable are those which retain youthful characteristics, and in turn those qualities reflect one of the deepest features of the human mind.

So let us look at the thursic side of that Aeon.

Here's one example of something I hope I am not alone in being sick to the teeth of: adults using baby talk.

The other week, I read a report of a magistrate doing the requisite telling-off thing to a woman described as 'heavily pregnant' for an alcohol related offence. The admonishment actually went, 'You've got a baby in your tummy...'

Yes, this is a magistrate we're talking about here, not some soppy teenage twit who gets a warm glow inside from saying the word 'tummy'.

Did she think the woman she was addressing was severely intellectually retarded? Aren't magistrates supposed to be mature and sensible members of the community? Apparently 'no' is the answer to both of those questions.

Even professionals like doctors and vets use the word 'poo' these days, a perfectly suitable term for 8-year-olds, before they get the hang of what social contexts demand 'excrement' or 'faeces', and which demand 'crap' or 'shit'.

So what is this about, this infantile regression in an adult?

To cast the question wider: Why can't I jump on and off buses as they hang around in traffic? Is it because we can no longer stand to bruise a few idiots a year in exchange for these trivial freedoms? Are we thereby a more compassionate society?

That's the surface of it, that is what we are supposed to believe, but the rate at which the overprotection culture has conquered everything suggests a very strong economic driver. That driver is insurance; this is what makes sense of the extreme anti-smoking notices, which in some places even appear out of doors these days, in defiance of the idea of near-infinite dilution.

Harm is not the issue; the true logic of this idiocy is that some person might sue, and sue successfully, someone who allows smoke to drift over their home or business premises. After all, we are talking about a legal system that awarded a claimant against McDonalds for serving her the hot coffee she scalded herself with. I mean, I wouldn't mind seeing Mac's getting screwed into the middle of next week, but that decision has made the law into a moron, and one fears what such stupidity is capable of.

Thus, three thurses for thee, dear citizen, and not, like in the words of Skirnismal, 'lust, loathing and lechery', but things far filthier and much less fun: things that contribute vitally to the nourishment of the system we find ourselves in, the sordid details of the pathology of consumerism.

That was the first one: **Infantilization**. It is an Aeonic thurs, specific to the Aeon of Horus, the thursic side of the Child principle, which is in itself no better nor worse than the Mother or Father principles. All Aeons get corrupted, cheapened, vulgarized; monetized, to use one of the more revolting of contemporary expressions.

So we've isolated one horrible strand of modern politics and control: the Crowned and Conquering Brat, alive and kicking down the legal system. Let's pan out to the bigger picture:

The **BIG BOSS THURS—Consumerism;**

This is fed by a whole slew of demons:

First, **Control**:—This is a genuinely thursic force, one with no conscious side at all. William Burroughs had this one's number: Control doesn't operate rationally; its horizons are limited; hence it is a genuine thurs. Burroughs saw that it emerges from the fear of death and its appetite for more control is insatiable.

In a dialogue he conducted via cut-up trance, he asked:

'What does Control want?'

'More Control,' came the reply.

Control turns up in every society. It is an old whore, which will work for anybody stupid or desperate enough to employ it. It is not peculiar to our present age. Think of it like this: it forms the demand side of the economy of stupidity. In its present form, it is nourished and strengthened by Infantilization.

Let's look in more detail at infantilization. It's in full swing with our claim and blame culture, surely its epitome, the attitude that the adult citizen is not responsible, that Baby needs protecting from Hirself every second of every day.

What then is the function of infantilization?

It is to keep us grasping, grasping for more, like a spoiled, unloved child.

It is the slave of corporations and advertising, which exhort us to buy much more stuff than we need.

According to a survey done in the late '90s, it was at that time only about the first £10,000 of income that made a difference to our material happiness; below that level, we are genuinely poor. Above that level, income only impacts our happiness to the extent it is more or less than what others are earning.

In other words, many people work long hours at boring, pointless, unsatisfying jobs simply to achieve status. People sell their souls to work, to obtain something as ridiculous as relative financial status.

No wonder infantilization is necessary to drive consumerism; a truly grown-up person would not buy into such a crock of crap.

In a parallel and related development, you've probably noticed doctors getting more aggressive about health. Your health, that used to belong to you, to care for or abuse as you saw fit. Doctors have become as whiningly moralistic as priests, and the cult they are priests of is life-extension. This cult has become as powerful as the old priesthoods of morality and work. Recent attempts to destroy the free market in medicinal herbs is sold to the public on the basis of 'we know better than you do', but its real reason is obviously profit for big drug companies.

That link is part of a structural relationship: Infantilization is supported by:

Intellectual dishonesty.

This thurs has really come out of the closet lately; governments are getting shockingly blatant in their lying. A recent example—a few years ago, the UK government's chief drugs advisor, Prof David Nutt, was asked to come up with a scale of the harmfulness of drugs, both legal and illegal, based on objective, measurable quantities like hospital admissions.

He did so, and the government didn't like his findings. When Nutt defended them, they sacked him, saying that his scale of harmfulness—sanctified by scientific method—sent out the wrong message.

Let's run that past ourselves again: The truth, i.e. the best data we can get, sends out the wrong message. Such contempt for truth would be funny if it wasn't causing so much harm.

Another thurs that supports Control is:

Loss of trust in subjectivity.

We are living in an era where subjective reporting is not to be trusted. This of course links in to the embedded institutional distrust of people's behaviour and judgment, which in turn feeds into our disempowerment by the medical profession.

American writer Marilynne Robinson tackles this problem. In her book *Absence of Mind*,[33] she writes:

> *'A central tenet of the modern world view is that we do not know our own minds, our own motives, our own desires. And—as an important corollary—certain well-qualified others do know them. ... of the ... testimony of individual consciousness and experience among us, ... We have been persuaded that it is a perjured witness.'*

This reminds us of the mental violence done to the public by the arch-manipulators of the last century, particularly Edward Bernays and Emma Freud. Between them, these two demonized any inner authority humans might have and attacked autonomy and community, in order to reduce people to docile consumers. Where subjectivity is devalued, we have no position to fight from, no other source of authority to oppose the rapacity of government, big business and vested professional interests.

Robinson is coming from the humanities side of the argument, and the whole territory of the arts is threatened with trivialization by the anti-subjectivist position. That position is associated, with some accuracy, with the scientific attitude. You may have seen articles with titles such as 'Yes, we really do fall in love—brain scans prove it', as if subjective reports of feelings have no validity, and the objective measurements of science do.

So is Science then the enemy, the thursic force here?

---

[33] Robinson M. (2011). *Absence of Mind: The Dispelling of Inwardness from the Modern Myth of the Self*, Yale University Press.

Before going into that big question, I want to say that I'd really rather you didn't take my word for any of this. Check it out for yourself. Confront, immerse yourself in, question, every aspect of this modern world and determine which you can use, which you need artfully to avoid, and which are your sworn enemies.

And with all of them, understand how to transcend their influence. Even those you approve of, you will eventually need to learn how to overcome in yourself, because they represent partial truths.

Here's a personal example: a story of Science and me.

I remember vividly the moment I fell in love with science. It coincided with the first time I abandoned magical thinking. I was around 4, and my dad asked me what I wanted for my birthday. I replied: a magic wand, a real one, like Sooty's got, one that can do real magic. My dad told me then that magic wasn't real. I recall the moment precisely; we were facing a row of shops on a mundane street in the West London suburb I grew up in. At that point, something big happened inside me, and the next time I thought about that incident it was from the point of view of someone who had turned wholeheartedly towards science. Science represented power, and I had unknowingly launched myself into the mystery of the Faustian bargain, which underlies so much of modern Western history.

Many occultists, and even some magicians, believe that science is the enemy. It is not. Science is common sense, ordinary logic, in its most detailed form. It is foreign neither to our nature as human beings nor to the projects of personal power and initiation.

What is the enemy, has been called Scientism, alternatively *parascience*. The latter term was coined by Marilynne Robinson, and either term can be defined as the talking of science-like religious drivel.

I'll give you an example from a science writer I used to respect, Ben Goldacre. He critiques a parapsychology experiment which failed to demonstrate extraordinary powers; so far, so good—methodological criticism is part of the advancement of scientific knowledge.

But he is not satisfied with a mere technical critique; he wants people to stop conducting parapsychology experiments at all, because, quote, 'we know that ESP is not real'.

Do we? That sounds like a religious position to me; it is certainly not a scientific one.

Scientism is a very special thurs, another one that is peculiar to the Aeon of Horus. We have rejected the religions of the monotheist Aeon, but we can't do without big, simplifying, stupid statements about the nature of the universe, so we form a new one. Scientism is a rather shabby attempt at a religion, and it is practised by a highly vocal subculture, the best-known member of which is Richard Dawkins.

Dawkinsites have constructed an argument which is superficially like science, but lacks it rigour. They have descended to a religious position that owes everything to Christianity's simplistic monochrome, in its energetic denial of some part or other of the human being, in its sterile inability to embrace the totality of what human experience is. They take science as their starting point, but then go way beyond its remit, much further than the evidence warrants, to present their hysterical-sounding denials. They are cops, patrolling the limits of reality with big sticks, falsely labelled 'Scientific Reason'.

Robinson writes:

> *'...the polemical impulse to assert the authority of science, understandable when the project was relatively new... is by now an atavism that persists as a consequence of this same polemical impulse.'*

And further:

> *'A difference between ... science and parascience, is the desire in the latter case to treat scientific knowledge as complete, at least in its methods and assumptions, in order to further the primary object of closing questions about human nature...'*

That pretty much pins down the thursic nature of Scientism: the closing off of questions which have in no way been adequately addressed by science. The old separation into 'non-overlapping magisteria' is under attack from Scientism, and the flavour of this discourse is a shallow triumphalism, a territorial pissing match by scientists who have blundered into areas that their discipline is not competent to address.

True science is at home in the real universe, which is chaotic and open-ended. However, devotees of the Scientism faith, such as Dawkins and Goldacre, are deeply uncomfortable about that lack of closure; they are seeking faith in order and closure. Either they have no insight into their own thinking or they are being dishonest about the fact that they are seeking faith.

The confusion of science with Scientism is greatly to the benefit of Scientism, whose adherents would love us to think they were talking real science, and it has led some magical writers to attempt to justify magical thinking by invoking the radical relativism of postmodern philosophers.

Whilst I salute the intention behind such attempts, I remain unimpressed by such short-cuts to magical belief as the following:

> *'... if everything we believe about the world is an arbitrary, socially-constructed symbol; if nothing inherently means anything; if reality itself—as many postmodernists claim—is just a collection of such arbitrary symbols, then*

magic becomes not only possible, but inevitable.'

That's a quote from *Postmodern Magic*, by Patrick Dunn.

The trick Dunn is using here seems to be to degrade the objectivity-status of consensus reality in order to make it more vulnerable to magic. We might call this the Chemotherapy Ploy: with cytotoxic drugs, we hope they will poison the cancer cells rather faster than the healthy host cells. Similarly, with PoMo anti-science we attack consensus reality, in the hope that the 'irrationalism' of magic gets a foothold before our universe crumbles into total incoherence.

Postmodern philosophy brought in a breath of liberating ideas, especially in analysing how philosophical positions are affected by the social reality of the writer. However, some of these tendencies have become profoundly toxic and downright silly where they've tried to deal with scientific epistemology.

PoMo critiques of physical science have delivered tools into the hands of the religious ultra-right, who are only too glad to be told that the theory of biological evolution (one of the scientific theories most consistently supported by the evidence), is just another possible viewpoint, to be placed alongside non-scientific views like Creationism. The PoMo science agenda also benefits the rapacious corporations and their political puppets who would squirm out from under the mountain of evidence for global warming.

Anyone who is still mucking about with PoMo anti-science drivel would do well to read theoretical physicist Alan Sokal's critiques of that tendency's worst excesses. In 1996, Sokal's article 'Transgressing the boundaries: Towards a transformative hermeneutics of quantum gravity' was accepted, and published in all seriousness by the prestigious American cultural studies journal *Social Text*. After its publication, Sokal 'fessed up to the hoax, declaring that every statement in that article was either 'trivial, nonsensical or meaningless', provoking a storm of often-acrimonious debate. One of the more delightful exchanges to emerge from this brouhaha was when one of the editors of *Social Text* declared that Sokal was 'under-educated' in the branch of philosophy he was critiquing; one of Sokal's supporters asked that editor: 'How does it feel to be duped by the under-educated?'

Basically, we don't need some hippy-dippy paradigm shift in order to fight Scientism—all we need is clear thinking.

Let's go a layer deeper: much misunderstanding of what science is, is underpinned by confused notions of what materialism really is.

'Materialism' is often blamed by 'magicians' for the state modern culture is in. Is that fair? Is Materialism a thurs?

One understanding of the word, in which it means 'obsession with owning more stuff', is totally thursic. This pathology is better thought of as consumerism, which I discussed above. Consumerism is of course underpinned by the Scientistic denial that there is any reality other than the external stuff we can measure; why should we seek anything except money and goods if inner states are not really real?

However, this position is actually pseudo-materialism, and is definitively demolished by British philosopher Galen Strawson. He writes:

> *'To be ... a genuine, realistic materialist, is to hold that experiential phenomena ... are part of this total physical existence.'*

So REAL materialism does not equal reductionism. Strawson writes:

> *'When I say that the mental, and in particular, the experiential, is physical, and endorse the view that 'experience is just neurons firing', I mean something completely different from what some materialists have apparently meant by saying such things. I don't mean that all aspects of what's going on in the case of conscious experience can be described by current physics ... Such a view amounts to some kind of ... 'eliminativism' with respect to consciousness and is certainly false. My claim is quite different. It is that the experiential considered specifically as such ... just is physical. No one who disagrees with this claim is a serious or remotely realistic materialist. One might put the point by saying that real materialism is not reductive... It doesn't claim that experience is anything less than we ordinarily conceive it to be, but that matter is more than we ordinarily conceive it to be.'*

This materialistic monism is very close to panpsychism, which Strawson admits as his personal belief, and continues:

> *'... real-materialism involves full acknowledgement of the reality of experiential phenomena. Experiential phenomena are as real as rocks...'*

No, real materialism, properly understood, is not eliminative of consciousness; it is not thursic; its thursic face is a subset of Scientism, which we've already dealt with.

So, we have isolated our Three Thurses, our toxic triad:

At the top, Consumerism.

This is fed by Infantilization and Scientism.

So, finally, how do we work against—or with—these entities?

Thurses we must fight; that is the nature of the path of consciousness. We must resist, critique, undermine and sabotage these forces of rampant stupidity. That is a life's work, and I wish you all persistence and luck in doing so.

However, some of the forces we've been considering are not thurses, but Etins. Science, in both its methodology and its results, can be seen as

Etinic. As Odin knew, Etins can give wisdom—as long as we are cautious and cunning in dealing with them.

In the Eddic poem *Vafthrudnismal*, Odin, disguised as Gagnrath, must show that he has some wisdom too, or Vafthrudnir will not be interesting in playing the game. The questions Gagnrath has are cosmological ones—it is not hard to imagine him as a cosmologist, questioning the universe through scientific procedures—he asks about moon and sun, about the origins of the universe.

"Tell me an eighth, Vafthruthnir,
since they say you are wise, and that you know:
what is your first memory, your earliest knowledge,
since you are wise, ettin?"
"In the endless winter,
before the shaping of the world,
Bergelmir was born..."

But in the end, Odin succeeds through a ruse:

"Far have I fared, much have I dared
oft have I tested the Regin.
What did Odin say to the ears of his son
before he was hoisted to the pyre?"
"No man knows that which you spoke
to your son in the days of yore.
It was with a doomed mouth
that I told old staves and spoke of Ragnarok.
Now I have exchanged my wisdom
in words with Odin. You are the wisest."

Odin wins by insisting on the primacy of the subjective: the answer to the riddle he poses is owned solely by himself. He values the wisdom he obtains from Vafthrudnir, but not to the extent of wanting to drown in it and lose himself. In the end, his own life, his own continuation as a principle of higher consciousness, must be valued above scientific knowledge. This is where Odin's approach differs from that of a scientist caught in the shallow illusions of Scientism. He is the living principle of higher consciousness, so he must never lose sight of those higher perspectives. To do so would be to forfeit his life, lost forever in Vafthrudnir's vasty halls, and that is his lesson to us in dealing with Etins.

RUNA Magazine and Recent Northern Mysteries Writings

Part 3 is shorter than the other parts because most of the Northern Mysteries articles I wrote were published in *Runa* magazine, and they later found their way into my *Bright From The Well* so they're not reprised here. *Runa* magazine was Ian Read's creation. Ian was editor of *Chaos International* magazine from Issue 6 to the end of the series, towards the end of which time he launched *Runa* magazine and edited its 24 issues, from 1997 to 2009. Ian is someone who has done a tremendous amount for the UK magical scene, but because he has not written much, and renown tends to be proportional to literary output, is a lot less well-known that many others who have done far less. *Runa* magazine's masthead mission was 'Exploring Northern European Myth, Mystery and Magic', and featured a wide variety of contributions from all sorts of magicians, artists and poets.

For those who wish to dive deeper into my Northern Mysteries writings, here are a few resources:

On the November New Moon in 2018 I started a blog for new writings of Rune-Gild members, which we've now taken down—most of my contributions to it, together with other material of mine and lots of other great stuff, can be found on the European Rune-Gild website.[34]

My course on Runic Sorcery can be found in Chaotopia School of Magic, an online school with a selection of other courses.[35]

In 2022 I contributed to a book which includes all the old rune-poems and a number of recently-written ones—*Rune-Poems: The Reawakened Tradition*. I have two poems in it, one for the Elder Futhark, written in 2008, and one for the Younger Futhark, written in 2021.[36]

In July 2020 Ingrid Fischer died. Her Master Work of Rune-Lore was a book, *Germanic Psychology,* for which she was recognized as Master in the Gild. It is a major contribution to a modern understanding of the complex and subtle soul-lore of the old Norse, synthesized from the perspectives of someone trained in Jungian analysis. Until its recent publication it had only previously been circulated within the Gild community. I had the honour of writing a foreword to this first public edition, which will, I hope, finally see the light of day in 2023.

---

[34] https://rune-gild-europe.org/

[35] Chaotopia School of Magic, Introduction to Rune Magic https://www.udemy.com/course/introduction-to-rune-magic/

[36] Lee D. 'Rune-Poems: The Reawakened Tradition'. https://chaotopia.com/2022/03/15/the-rune-poems-a-reawakened-tradition/

Runic Spells

Much of my work in the Northern Mysteries was, and is, strongly influenced by my chaos magic background. One of the results of this is my use of Northern symbols in unfamiliar ways. To lead into the next part of the book, here are two early runic collage-spells, one for the exposure of wrongdoing and one for justice.

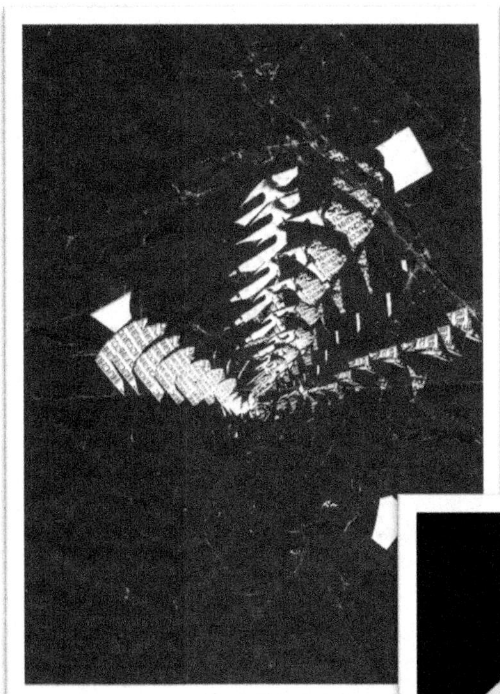

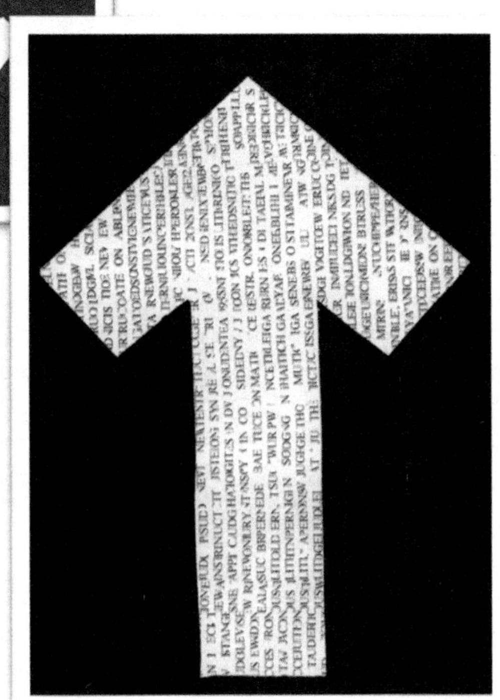

Part 4: Talks, Courses and Public Spells

Over the years I've written, co-created, and presented what must amount to hundreds of rituals at IOT and IOT-adjacent events. The co-creation thing has long been one of the IOT's specialities—people often turn up with only a vague idea of what they want to do, so together we design and enact a working on the spot. Newcomers are drawn into the process of ritual planning right from the start. This becomes a sort of accelerated training in group magic.

Then there are workings and talks which I've presented to the public. My first talk to a rather larger audience—maybe 100 or so—was at UKAOS 1992. UKAOS was an early manifestation of the chaos scene in London, running from 1992 to '95. The size of the audience occasioned my first attack of stage fright: I looked out at the assembled crowd and my left leg started vibrating back and forth. I didn't really want to start my presentation while I was looking like that, so I put my script down and fiddled about with the lectern until I found a balance point where the shaking stopped. Once I'd found the right posture, the freed-up energy rushed through me like a bolt of electricity, which was a nice start to the talk.

Why do we do public magic? Well, for the obvious reasons—to educate, to push our personal agendas and to have fun. But beyond that, there's a desire to change the wider world. When we use magic that way, it becomes what I called the 'poor man's sword' in my Younger Futhark poem:

NAUTH ᚾ nauðr ("need")
Need's the fire 'neath wizard's pot
Nightside art's the poor man's sword, when
Naught'll do but sculpt a lot and
Nail his soul to carven board.
Narrowed fire is fierce, do not
Neglect the power of straitened word.
Nothing breaks the grip of lack like
Need itself turned on its back.

This use of magic also opens up the old question of the role of the magician in the world.

I've been asking 'What is magic for?' since I started with it. I used that question as the title of my talk at the 1987 Chaos Symposium, where I shared a stage with Pete Carroll, Ralph Tegtmeier and Freya Aswynn.

My answer at that stage was deliberately multiple. My whole magical career has been an arc of articulation of the various strands that make up my magical life, strands which aren't explicitly united anywhere in the published magical culture. It's not easy to give a pat answer. But I'm going to frame that question again, and look at how we think we can use magic to improve the condition of the world.

What does it mean to be a wizard?

At one time, it was an outsider who, paradoxically, served the community: the shaman, the spirit-whisperer, the death-and-birth specialist.

Then it was an underground person, scapegoated, persecuted, a so-called witch, marginalized, using magic to scrape by in a hostile world, practising small spells for small change.

What about now? What do we contemporary persons who identify as magicians actually do?

In the early years of my magical career it was all training and tentative approaches to group work. Spells were for our own concerns and to develop our magic. We were getting more proficient at gaining the resources we needed to do our will in the world. We helped our friends and family with spells for health, resources, security, justice and so on.

Now, alongside the spells, we cultivate energy, life force, athm, to stay healthy and prolong life. And of course we spend more time doing healing magic, as we and our friends get older and frailer.

And beyond all that, we see things in the world that are wrong. As an exercise in adopting very unusual perspectives, you might ask yourself: What sort of person looks at the world and says, yeah, that's totally fine? When a magician wakes up to magic then they are bound to find that they want to change the world, and it seems self-evident to me that you can't live your best life in a broken society, or at least, not unless you're engaged in doing your best to improve it.

There's a long tradition of magicians meddling in world affairs—check out Arkon Daraul's classic popular study *Secret Societies,* which depicts magicians as grey eminences secretly guiding the evolution of the world. And Peter Carroll stated that the mission of the order he founded, the IOT, was twofold:

> *The Pact has but two aims. Firstly the pursuit of the Great Work of Magic and pleasures and profits attendant to this Quest. Secondly to act as a*

Psychohistoric Force in the Battle for the Aeon.

However, that is a very broad and arguable remit; the Aeon we envisage is not going to be the same for all of us. I would imagine there's quite a gulf between the Aeon as Carroll understands it and the Aeon of most IOT members.

As for my own involvement in magic-for-the-world there was an explicit sense in which the Phoenix Light workings (I mention them right near the start of Part 1, under *Lamp of Thoth*) were to bring illumination to all, but there was no practical work for or against particular things in the world. The first magic I recall doing for a particular world issue was the anti-nuke sigil we did for the TV in 1987, which I wrote about in Part 1. Another was in 1994, when William Burroughs, Frater Dahlfar 23, networked through the organization for magical help to deal with a hysterically anti-gay 'Christian' group called the Westboro Baptist Church. These were one of those warped strains of 'Christianity' that are focused on hate, led by a cult patriarch called Fred Phelps. They kept turning up at book launches and aggressively heckling any gay authors they could find. We had a degree of success—after the workings, Frater Dahlfar told us Phelps's gang got run out of a nearby town by a jeering crowd.

In this section I talk about those sorts of workings, and others I worked with the Discordian community. My own drive towards such engagement started way back: as a teenage anarchist I'd already reached that familiar stage of despair with mainstream politics. Even then it was clear how corrupt it was, how we cannot expect elected officials to do what they were put there for. For a while, I placed my hope in the sort of anarchism that involved communal living. Then I stumbled into a political discourse that seemed to promise more useful perspectives: on one of my early acid trips, a rather challenging one, the unpleasant craziness began to crystallise into something better when my friend Ben thrust a zine into my hands. It was a copy of *King Mob Echo*, the mag of the Notting Hill Gate Situationists. In it were passages about the end of culture. I felt like something inside me was burning away into pure energy; I'd discovered nihilism and lit a bonfire under my whole idea of culture and what it is for.[37]

Later, I found out more about the author of the piece that had set me on fire—Raoul Vaneigem. The passage was a quote from his book *The Revolution in Everyday Life*. This was another important linkage for me—maybe in the language of Situationism was a new approach, something that

[37] 'Culture is not your friend' - Terence McKenna

could make the world better from another direction... I was groping my way towards a magical approach to improving the world.

And what is it we are actually doing with world-changing magic these days? What common features can we pick out?

One is that modern activist magic is mostly done online. Some actual physical-plane demonstrations at some site or other are attended by practising magicians, wielding their spells, but most spellcasting these days is probably done on Facebook, Mastodon, Instagram and even, I am told, on TikTok.

This kind of magic obviously works on more than one level: if you post a 'meme' picture or sigil on social media, then it will function as an affirmation of a particular activist position in the minds of those who see it, as well as performing (or failing at) whatever more esoteric pathway it was designed for.

People who have grown up with social media are obviously more at ease with it than my generation are, and I suspect that the hit-and-miss nature of social media communication (the Alzheimer's-like amnesia of Facebook's algorithms, the ever-present Aeon of War and Vengeance tripwires of Twitter, even when it had responsible management, most of one's feed being adverts in Instagram) is something we oldsters have less patience with. However, just because a system or idea or institution is limited, imperfect, even corrupt, aspects of it might still be usable for positive change.

Which aspects? The key here is probably quantity. You're hoping that your meme will be seen by as many eyes as possible, so that it has the highest probability of finding a sympathetic and magically effective mind behind those pupils.[38]

What about the actual magical dynamics? Back in the early days of group chaos magic we worked out that the Austin Spare model of how sigils work needed updating. In that model, we each create a sigil and by progressively abstracting from a written or depicted desire, until what we have drawn no longer looks anything like the original picture or words. We then imprint the sigil in a moment of vacuity, of gnosis, and it works because part of us knows what it's for, and that part makes sure it works without the interference of the conscious mind.

But what if you don't know what it's for? What if someone hands you a sigil and asks you to charge it? We experimented with what we called 'Bring

[38] 'Meme': I'll drop the scare quotes now. That was a tribute to the original idea, before it came to mean a little picture on social media, and meant a concept or tune or little picture which grabs your attention. It was coined by Richard Dawkins. The idea itself, a self-perpetuating element of language, was originated by William S Burroughs and called a word-virus.

a Sigil Parties', where a circle of us did exactly that—passed our sigils on to our neighbour before starting the gnosis part of the working, so that everyone was charging another person's sigil. We got a consistently high level of success, which demonstrated that some part of us knowing what the sigil is for is entirely unnecessary. We're closer here to Alan Chapman's model of magical action in *Advanced Magick for Beginners*:[39] basically, all you need to do is to believe that some set of actions you perform will result in the outcome you intend. This model of magic makes the widespread dissemination of a sigil a worthwhile thing to experiment with.

So we can put a sigil or symbol out there for people to use. But how scaleable is magic? I went to a small meeting some years ago that was aimed at getting some sort of widespread magical actions going. We ended up debating whether magic can be treated as a technology sufficiently precise and simple so as to be able to do such a thing.

We were a group of IOT members who'd been invited along; our hosts, activists for a kind of Transhumanism, seemed convinced it could. We were convinced otherwise, from group magical experience. It can't just be a case of handing out spell recipes to the troops; there has to be some experience, some self-training first, and hardly anybody wants to go through the training exercises of magic. Magicians are a self-selecting minority.

But then again, when lots of people work magic together, there are some complex feedback mechanisms and energy phenomena which ramp things up. I've seen a 'group gnosis amplification effect' ever since I started coaching CBW in groups. The first time I really took notice of it was early in my breathwork career, when I went to a weekend retreat. I had a full-blown mystical experience, the first time such a thing happened to me on nothing but connected breathwork. I sat up from a session where about ten other people had also been doing the breathwork, and I saw a haze of light connecting the auras of everyone present. I stepped out into the garden and that was it, a full experience of unity with the world. OK, so we'd been doing a lot of breathwork and talking intensively about some of our stuff. That will have laid the foundations for the way our energies interacted and synergized, but the moment itself seemed to arise from the fact that we were all in an enhanced state, an ESC or gnosis, at the same time in the same place.

That was a concentrated experience of what happens to some extent in a good group magical working. The effects are much more than simply additive; there is a multiplication of the intensity of the gnosis. As I mentioned, I think physical proximity is important to this effect, and I've never experienced such intensity in an online group. The Energy Magic

[39] Chapman A. (2008). *Advanced Magick for Beginners*, Aeon Books.

weekend workshop I ran for Occulture Berlin in 2021 came closer than I'd imagined possible, but there is no way this could have amounted to the kind of scaleability our Transhumanist friends would have liked. There are a number of reasons for that, one of which is that the anecdotes I've just related concerned groups of people of whom *a good proportion were very experienced* in magic and enhanced states.

Returning to online spells, some people have another layer of magical thinking about the mechanisms: the idea that we are at the dawn of machine sentience, and that the Internet is one huge, gargantuan half-conscious critter, a technological Ymir about to be carved into truly sentient enclaves by magically-inspired technologists. It might be worth engaging with that belief for the purpose of some spells...

Over the last fifteen or so years we've seen an explosion in social media. This has served to show us how symbols can be hijacked and transvalued. Agitprop artists and Situationists in the 1950–60s had subverted, *détourned* the symbols of the dominant culture into something that undercut their significance, and something like this continued into the work of artists such as Ivan Stang who created the *Church of the Sub-Genius*. Well, something very like that was happening with our own magical symbols—a symbol almost indistinguishable from the good ol' chaos star was suddenly being utilized by far-right Russian nationalists.

These last few years have meant magicians have had to learn some new lessons about public communication, including the fact that your community becomes invisible if it isn't posting on social media. The IOT began life as a relatively secretive organization, which worked fine in the pre-web era, when people would find you by word of mouth or pub meetings or bookshops. But in the online era, this meant that people were not seeing any evidence of us in the public world, and it appears that some people actually thought we'd become defunct. This is very far from the case: the British Isles IOT is more active, vital and creative than I've seen it for years, and attracting exceptional people into the community.

Here's a particularly dark public spell, my first bit of media demonology:

The Inferno of Choronzon, 1996

I put this rite together for public performance with the help of the extraordinary Frater Remarkable, who did the audio tracks. I can still hear his 'Death Choppers of the Apocalypse', on a paranoid day. The working was a vortex of apocalyptic imagery and violent ethical confusion, opposing extreme viewpoints being shouted out by the demonic Chorus, as participants were formed into a human triangle into which the demons of the media were invoked. At the climax of the working, the triangle burst open into liberation. The performance in Los Angeles went pretty well, but then I flew from LA to Seattle and presented it again. That was the wildest and most intense public ritual I'd then done. This was an audience who were really up for intensity, much more enthusiastic than the jaded LA crowd. We went from an arena of competitive entertainment to a culture of collective ecstasy.

After that amazing weekend I went with two other magicians to visit William Burroughs at his home in Lawrence, Kansas. After that three-day magical meeting we were in that wide-open state that comes from magical intensity and sleep-deprivation, and we flew from Seattle to Kansas City. We boarded the plane, and the captain introduced himself as... Captain Clark! All of us had read Burroughs's account of how he came upon the '23 synchronicities' as a result of two deadly disasters involving captains with that name, so there was more than a frisson of mortal dread mingled with the sheer euphoria of synchronicity as the plane soared up into the towering black clouds of a storm front...

THE INFERNO OF CHORONZON: AHPERL 548, 1996

PURPOSE:

This is a Rite of Illumination and Self-Enchantment, the object of which is to bring participants into sharp awareness of their core values, and to empower these with the gnosis of the primal energies underlying the media's representations of Hell.

INTRODUCTION

The Rite uses the symbolism of the Four Horsemen as the bringers of Death as seen on Death TV. The violent images of the TV screen are imprinted in the flesh, pushing the passive viewer towards standardized thought, standardized emotional response, image made flesh, word made flesh.

The 4 Horsemen are the riders of the endless apocalypse, stalking the world barely below the conscious level.

The realm of the media is the Inferno of Choronzon, the Demon of the Abyss of Hallucination. We will recapitulate these images under magical conditions, rending the veil of illusion, and plunging into the basal layer of primitive impersonal terror underlying the images. This is the Abyss, where the Great Old Ones or Archons of terror surge up from the depths of our being. These Archons are the primal forces of the instincts, of the first two neurogenetic circuits,[40] corresponding to a vision of fear and greed on a cosmic scale.

The participants will be stood in a Triangle, with the Principal Officers at the corners. The sound images will generate a series of 'virtual doorways', around the Triangle. The rite climaxes with the quotes at the end shouted out at random by the principal officers.

RUNNING SEQUENCE

Everyone to get into Triangle, arms linked.

The INVOCATION: [With thanks to Frater Dahlfar 23, aka William S. Burroughs]

(*Audio*: Coil's 'How to Destroy Angels')

To the Ancient Ones, to the Lord of Abominations, Humwawa, whose face is a mass of entrails, whose breath is the stench of dung and the perfume

[40] See Timothy Leary's Eight Circuit Model of consciousness, and its development by Robert Anton Wilson. See also my use of it in *Chaotopia!*.

of decay, dark angel of all that is excreted and sours, lord of decay, lord of the future, who rides on a whispering south wind,

to Pazuzu, lord of fevers and plagues, dark angel of the four winds with rotting genitals from which he howls through sharpened teeth over stricken cities

to Kutulu, the sleeping serpent who cannot be summoned,

to the Akhkharu, who suck the blood of men since they desire to become men

to the Lalussu, who haunt the places of men

to Gelal and Lilit, who invade the beds of men and whose children are born in secret places,

to Addu, raiser of storms who can fill the night sky with brightness,

to Malah, lord of courage and bravery,

to Zahgurim, whose number is 23 and who kills in an unnatural fashion,

to Zahrim, a warrior among warriors,

to Itzamna, spirit of early mists and showers,

to Ix Chel, the spider-web-that-catches -the-dew-of-morning,

to Zuhuy-Kak, virgin fire

to Ah Dziz, the master of cold,

to Kak U Pacat, who works in fire,

to Ix Tab, goddess of ropes and snares, patroness of those who hang themselves,

to Schmuun, the silent one, twin brother of Ix Tab,

to Xolotl the unformed, lord of rebirth,

to Aguchi, master of ejaculations,

to Osiris and Amen in phallic form,

to Hex Chun Chan, the dangerous one,

to Ah Pook the destroyer,

to the Great Old One and the Star Beast,

to Pan, god of panic,

to the nameless gods of dispersal and emptiness,

to Hassan i Sabbah, master of assassins

Nothing is true/everything is permitted.

THE HORSEMEN

First upon the scene is FAMINE: the waters are rising, flooding the coastal plains, pushing the still-swelling population up the hillsides, deserts advance, the migrants overrun the fertile land... all you can hear are the silent pleas of the starving, a low wail as the soundtrack to a dying world... the soil itself is dying... exhausted people haunt an exhausted planet...

Where are you in all this, what constitutes the wealth of your life that you can stand outside this picture. Is it money? Is it intelligence? Or is it mere luck?

What are your values in all this? What do you want to propel your life towards?

Now we are joined by PESTILENCE, bringing images of the rapid death by Ebola, the slow wasting of AIDS victims, plague striking down Indian cities as the doctors flee to relative safety… the buzzing of insects feeding off human decay, the stink of disinfectant and faeces, the sounds of choking and vomiting, the destruction of the flesh. An image of an airport lounge, a woman in a queue collapses screaming, silver dust pouring from her empty eye sockets... a new virus has arrived... no-one is outside the range of these new viruses.

Where are you in all this? How come you are not sick? Is it because of drugs—but they cannot be invented fast enough to control these new illnesses, and most of them are useless anyway. Is it intelligence? Knowledge? Magic, maybe?

What do you want, what is it that will keep you full of vitality, what are your values in all this?

Now we are watching live WAR, images of Rwanda, lakes clogged with rotting corpses, the sound of gunfire, rioting, fanaticism, revolution. These images form a deathcamp of the soul, the killing fields on which the last vestiges of Christian sentiment lay dying, the butcher's slab of liberation.

How did you escape war? Was it luck again? What are your values in all this? Where is your aggression? What world do you want to create?

Finally we encounter DEATH itself, the programme written in us that defeats all our aspirations, or brings us our final glory. People sit in their little houses, slowly killing themselves. A stench of silence, of acquiescence, the death of passion and curiosity. The ante-room to the cancer ward of quiet despair. One of the walls is ashen grey, and it is pierced by the skeletal toe of a gigantic Death figure, his scythe descending in the blue flicker of the TV light, scything through the useless dead flesh, the pathetic half-lives, the boredom and futility of these blinks of existence.

You have made your choice, or you would not be here: You have chosen to live fully rather than die slowly. But how? What are the values that keep you alive?

IF YOU DO NOT DECIDE WHAT YOU WANT, SOMEONE ELSE WILL DECIDE FOR YOU!

Pause for a moment, and imagine you are going to die in one month's time. What will hold your life together in that month?

THE CHORUS:

WHEN WALKING IN OPEN TERRITORY, BOTHER NO-ONE. IF SOMEONE BOTHERS YOU, ASK HIM TO STOP. IF HE DOES NOT STOP, DESTROY HIM.

SATAN REPRESENTS KINDNESS TO THOSE WHO DESERVE IT, INSTEAD OF LOVE WASTED ON INGRATES.

SATAN REPRESENTS VENGEANCE INSTEAD OF TURNING THE OTHER CHEEK

DO UNTO OTHERS AS THEY DO UNTO YOU

KNOW THAT YOU ARE WORKING ON ANOTHER LEVEL ENTIRELY FROM THE REST OF THE WORLD

LEX TALIONIS—JUSTICE IS SERVED BY FANG AND CLAW

SMASH THE CRUMBLING CROSS, FOR MIGHT IS RIGHT, LET THE SHUFFLING ZOMBIES GROPE FOR LIGHT

THERE IS NO BOND THAT CAN UNITE THE DIVIDED BUT LOVE, ALL ELSE IS A CURSE

Now breathe in the stench of a world's insanity, breathe in Death, breathe in Plague, breathe in War, breathe in Famine... feel the force of your feelings, feel the fierce bloodlust of killing, feel the nausea, feel the fear, feel the pain, feel the anger, feel the violence, feel the old itch of death in your soul... And now you hang in the Abyss of Choronzon, your flesh swarming with the madness of humanity, the sheer force of the Great Old Ones, your mind seething with a torrent of doubt or the coherent beam of certainty.

THESE ARE DEAD, THESE FELLOWS, THEY FEEL NOT. WE ARE NOT FOR THE POOR AND SAD, THE LORDS OF THE EARTH ARE OUR KINSFOLK

WE HAVE NOTHING WITH THE OUTCAST AND UNFIT. LET THEM DIE IN THEIR MISERY

COMPASSION IS THE VICE OF KINGS. STAMP DOWN THE WRETCHED AND THE WEAK; THIS IS THE LAW OF THE STRONG

YE ARE AGAINST THE PEOPLE, O MY CHOSEN

DEEM NOT OF CHANGE—THE SLAVES SHALL SERVE

I WILL BRING YOU TO VICTORY AND JOY; I WILL BE AT YOUR ARMS IN BATTLE AND YE SHALL DELIGHT TO SLAY

If you have your core values clear in your mind, let them be flooded with the blind force of the Archons. If you are confused, let the power of the Archons rise up into your seething mind, until a glyph or series of glyphs forms.

I SUGGEST A WAR AGAINST STUPIDITY

WHY BE DEPRESSED, DUMB AND AGITATED WHEN YOU CAN BE HAPPY, SMART AND TRANQUIL?

IF STUPIDITY DECREASED, LESS MONEY WOULD BE WASTED ON VAST ORGANIZED IMBECILITIES SUCH AS THE ARMS RACE, AND MORE WOULD BE AVAILABLE FOR LIFE-ENHANCING PROJECTS

A WORTHWHILE GOAL IS THE ABOLITION OF STARVATION AND POVERTY

YOU WILL PROBABLY LIVE A LOT LONGER THAN YOU EXPECT

NOBODY IS UNIMPORTANT ANY MORE

A MAN MUST DESTROY HIMSELF BEFORE OTHERS CAN DESTROY HIM

IF THE WORLD SEEMS TO BE GETTING SMALLER AND NASTIER ALL THE TIME, THEN YOUR STUPIDITY IS STEADILY INCREASING

In either case, let the darkness show you the sigil of your deepest desires. Let your being be lit by this one spark of light. This is the deathless sigil that will accompany you on your next transformation, reappearing in your flesh as you hurtle across the Abyss.

Release!

Undreaming the Apocalypse

These days, much of what the groups I'm involved with do is about nudging the probabilities of the world towards a less desperate state. The situation is, I think you'd agree, much worse in many ways than it was in 1996. In 2020 I decided to create a new piece, to undo the apocalypse. This was in response to an art project I was invited to take part in, which seems to have run aground, but I used the core idea in a 2022 working, to undo the fixation on dramatized collapse that this culture has developed.

The details of that ritual are not included; this was a private working, but it involved a chaotron and the introductory script was as follows:

THE PURPOSE OF THIS WORKING

We need a deep and far-reaching shift in public narrative. There is too much focus on imagined dystopias, ideas that push people into helplessness.

I wrote two dystopian novels and I'm over dystopias now. I'd like to think I'm not alone.

The fantasy of apocalypse doesn't stand up to historical scrutiny. Cultures don't just collapse into nothing overnight—there's a long period of adoption of new perspectives, and we are at the start of something like that as the old order dies out. New narratives are developing in the shell of the old world, and we can help this process by opposing the tendency in the mass media to emphasize the dystopian dark side of that process.

Let's dismantle the mass media apocalypse fantasy.

THE MATERIALS OF THIS WORKING

I made conscious the apocalyptic nature of the media world 26 years ago. What better way to reverse the apocalypse than to use a reversed version of that working. The sound file for this working consists of reversed versions of the original audio from 1996.

And now, for a total change of vibe.

Working with Eris Discordia

The 2010s revival of Discordianism, another current that owes most of its popularity to Robert Anton Wilson, has generated a fresh artistic and occultural stream in the UK, including Festival 23 and the revival of the late 1960s idea of Arts Labs, community-based radical art collectives, spearheaded by Alan Moore in Northampton and since taken up in Liverpool, Sheffield, Teesside, South London and other places.

Since Festival 23, Anwen Fryer and I founded 'Magic, Witchcraft, Chaos and Beyond' and started presenting talks and workshops in the temple room above her Sheffield shop, 'Airy Fairy'.[41] When the lockdowns started, we moved it online. Some of the public magic I've been working in recent years has brought together IOT members and Discordians in a fruitful bit of networking over issues we can do magic for.

Much of the online magical teaching I do these days is for people who've come to magic via the Discordian scene. There seems to have been a boom in magical interest in the last two years, with more people coming into my favourite magical organizations and buying magic books in my friend's local bookshop. This is the kind of periodic shift in popular culture that Lionel Snell predicts with his Four Cultures model (see in particular *My Years of Magical Thinking*).[42] Of course, everything we humans do has (at least) two sides to it: this is the healthy and constructive side of a boom in magical thinking, just as the stupid side is the boom in daft ideas (so-called 'conspiracy theories') which is basically magical thinking with the critical perspective turned off.

So why do people choose to work with Eris, to honour and call upon Her? After all, She does have a reputation as a troublemaker, and Her best-known exploit involves disruption of a wedding party because She wasn't invited. But we don't have to dig down far to see that there's another side to that tale.

The wedding of sea-nymph Thetis and hero Peleus, to which the Olympian deities are invited, is a forced one. The bride Thetis is not the willing trophy of the arrogant hero, but a victim of rape, so there is a violent and dishonourable taint to the party right from the start. Eris is the bringer of truths the honoured deities don't want to hear.

---

[41] MWCB courses are announced in my newsletter, there's a link to subscribe at https://chaotopia.com/

[42] Lionel Snell's *My Years of Magical Thinking*, see my review at https://chaotopia-dave.blogspot.com/2017/02/my-years-of-magical-thinking-by-lionel.html

My own engagement with the idea of Eris included a little pilgrimage while my partner and I were at an event in the Pelion area. I got a nice apple, painted it gold and wrote *te kalliste* on it, as my offering. Right from the start, the journey was subject to chaotic influences—not only did we have some problems which led to serious delays before we even left England, but when we were there and planning the pilgrimage, we nearly went to the wrong place, due to a mis-transliteration of the local town Milina as Milies, which place is also on Pelion, but miles away.

It was worth the journey, for a number of reasons. For a start, it's easy to see why even demigods would pick this area for a wedding—a dramatic Palaeolithic cave, the Cave of Chiron, on a steep forested slope running down to the sea, headlands plunging to a semi-enclosed bay dotted with tiny islands.

We invoked Our Lady of Chaos. I left my golden apple sacrifice, then I turned back and photographed it. Immediately I knew that was not a good idea; this is when it became a bit more serious. This had to be a ritual from which I took nothing home with me, including any images of what I was leaving behind. I deleted the shot and felt better immediately.

The fact that deleting the shot seemed so important I take as a good sign: I was engaging more seriously with Eris. It is all too often easy to forget what is happening and default to mundanity.

Devotion to Eris is based on the fact that She is not a friend of sensible planning, or the kind of thinking that is based on the assumption that things are always going to be as they were. Of course, we humans need to live in that kind of world, it makes us feel secure, lowers our stress and conserves our energy. This planning attitude is our bread and butter mentation, and we identify with it, so that it becomes our dominant selfhood, our ego; which is why we take it personally and get annoyed when our plans go tits up.

But we are not always in control, not always living in a predictable world. We also need to be able to deal with confusing, complex situations, and quickly. This is a different kind of intelligence to that which assumes things and plans accordingly—this is the intelligence required to steer a speeding vehicle on a dangerous road in a sudden snowstorm. Or to innovate on the fly in situations where predicted and comfortable structures break down—say, to navigate social scenes involving anger or grief.

The Greeks had two words for time: *kronos*, which is the predictable, calendrical idea of time, and *kairos*, which is the moment of opportunity that requires an instant response, time as embodied immediacy. Kairos is depicted as a youth with a long forelock of hair, something you can seize him by. They also had a word for the cunning, fast intelligence that has the flexibility and lightness of touch to be able to seize the *kairos* when it presents itself—*metis*.

When we honour Eris, not only are we honouring life's chaos and unpredictability but we are also invoking *metis*, the cunning that will enable us to make the best out of the chaos that's going to happen at some stage whether we like it or not.

It seems this kind of approach to magic is not for all magicians. A few years ago, senior Chaos writer Peter Carroll opined in conversation that working with Eris had led to conflict in the ranks of the chaos magic world, so we should shift our allegiance to other deities. Not long after that, when Pete Carroll and Math Kaybrin's work *EPOCH*, with its beautifully drawn deity and elemental cards came out, the authors gifted our chaos group with a copy. We decided we would have to select a deity chaotically, to honour them using the new deck. A guest participant suggested we remove the Eris and Loki cards from the deck before doing so. Nobody else agreed—surely not inviting Eris (let alone Loki) is precisely what leads to trouble in the first place? So we went ahead with our random selection and, guess what, Eris's card came up, and we invoked Her.

This rejection of involvement with Eris seems to me to be a strange thought process for a magician: surely we honour Eris because we *know* that life is full of surprises, conflict and turnarounds? And surely such an attitude of stopping pretending that we are always in control can only be healthy. Discordians I know don't seem to be any more argumentative in their lives than any other magicians. Honouring the chaos and unpredictability of the world is also more likely to lead to experiences of fuller or 'higher' consciousness, in which we learn to see the world as it is, not as our expectations paint it. Someone who rejects Eris is resisting incursions of a fuller way of being, is resisting the recognition of chaos that is a necessary preliminary to any experience beyond the time-bounded (in the *kronos* sense) ego. An attitude to magic in which one always has to be in control is bound to lead to disappointment, reduction in general pleasure in life and, if pushed to its extreme, some sort of crisis in which the world proves to us that we cannot always be in the driving seat.

Eris might not always be a friendly face, but what deity is invariably friendly, if you look closely enough? Behind every deity's face is a facet of the cosmos as Other. If you engage with any deity deeply enough, your reward will be to see that totality gazing back at you. Maybe you will even recognize that gaze as a feature of your own divine nature. Eris's face is beautiful, frightening, awe-inspiring, humbling. Her frightening face is the face of the world when we have to acknowledge that we can no longer control it. Her joyous face is the world that opens up when we stop pretending we're in control because we are fed up with holding on so tight, and instead let go into what is happening and surf the chaos.

Festival 23

In late 2015 I was invited to join a group planning a Discordian festival in the Sheffield area.[43] I was the local published chaos magic author, so I was helping to plan the magical events. We had a meeting in a community room in town, and did a ritual to get the network (or 'NotWork' as the Discordians styled it) buzzing. It was an extraordinary opportunity to network with all sorts of interesting people, including members of what might be called the British psychedelic underground. The planned date for the festival clashed directly with another major magical meeting I would normally have gone to, so I decided I'd put the energy I'd have used for that event into the festival.

Anwen Fryer and I planned an opening ritual, with music by George Rogers, the intention of which was along the lines of: *We empower ourselves to put aside worn ideas and reality tunnels, find inspiration in each other, approach the weekend and the happenings with an open mind, and challenge comfort zones*. The secondary purpose of the ritual was to make sure that everyone who turned up knew this was a magical event.

Festival 23 was a single weekend in 2016 with 500 people. A good number of those joined in the ritual; for most of them it was the first time they'd got involved in such a thing. Two people formed an arch with raised arms, and whispered pre-arranged phrases to the participants as they approached the arch. The phrases included 'You are magical', 'You are creative', 'You are courageous', 'You are complete' and so on. The participants passed under the arch then joined it, forming their own arch. When everyone had formed arches, we started a chant of AAAAA (soft at first), everyone chanting in unison. During this, a manifestation of ERIS appeared and gave everyone a stirring pep talk.

The next day, I presented some hearty rune-song followed by introducing people to the psychedelic spirit Izawa (see below). The Festival was jam-packed with amazing events, installations, music, theatre and other stuff harder to classify, and ended on a stunning note. A couple of artists—I apologize for forgetting their names, it was that kind of a weekend—had built an installation for the final night, a Calvary cross formed of bookshelves. The shelves were crammed with self-help books. As people gathered for the final night, the cross of shelves was set on fire. People cheered, chanted, sang, generally whooped it up. Then a woman a few people away from me started singing England's unofficial national anthem—*Jerusalem*. The crowd took it up. It was a moment of intense emotion that was magical from the start, taking this stirring hymn with its lyrics by our greatest mystical poet, sung at

---

[43] Festival 23. https://festival23.org.uk/the-experience-2/

both the Labour Party conference and by Conservatives, and giving it a new energy, beyond the meanings it had accumulated.

Back in my youth I'd loved festivals, especially the free ones, but Festival 23 was something else. This particular weekend in a field was with people who mostly seemed to be involved in creating something. It was the polar opposite of consumer society. Discordianism had been well and truly reborn in the UK.

Burn, Wizard, Burn!

Another Discordian-adjacent magical current is money burning. Burning money can mean many things, but the core is surely that in such a monetized and debt-driven world it is a way to engage in a moment of magical and spiritual autonomy, a gnosis where you know you are beyond the shabby forces that appear most of the time to run the world. Jonathan Harris is a High Priest of this magical and religious gesture, and he runs a magazine devoted to it, *Burning Issue*.[44] Not to be confused with the professional firefighters' magazine of the same name!

I thought it was worth writing a lengthy review of this mag, partly to illustrate how magical the Discordian current is. The full piece is available on my blog;[45] here are a few of the main ideas from it:

> The way *Burning Issue* presents money burning underlines that magic is a basic layer of Discordianism's wing of the counterculture. There are some explicit magical references—my piece about sacrifice and magic for instance—but the magic in *Burning Issue* is more implicit and pervasive than that. Discordianism is one of the forms the counterculture has embraced this time round. A lot of what emerges into the public domain from that mix is artworks—performance, music, pictures, theatre and so on. These artists seem to be going beyond the slick, detached irony of PoMo and are at least tentatively edging into using magic as a core idea, and in some cases embracing it fully as a way of articulating what they are doing.
>
> This has to be the core of any counterculture now; other political mechanisms seem to be consistently failing to change the world in any human direction. When democracy is a casualty of 'post-truth', what is one to do, but some wizardry to help the messed-up world?
>
> Undo yourself with ecstatic states and stabilize those ecstasies with meditation, allowing insight into your divine-human nature to surface. Identify what runs you. Identifying and dismantling the false beliefs you've imprinted in trauma or just inherited from family and society gives you insight into how the world is made. You see behind the scenes of the world to how the stage-crews of your nervous system, your beliefs and the society you are embedded in make it all up. Having seen how it fits together, you have the insight to change it, to bring into this world, that is ever-dying and ever-being-born, better things. You can help to mend the world we are always breaking.

---

[44] *Burning Issue* https://www.burningissue.net/

[45] *Burning Issue* review - https://chaotopia-dave.blogspot.com/2018/12/burning-issue-worlds-first-magazine-for.html

This is magic.

Its tools include not only its public face of art-forms—pictures, films, performances—but the much vaster hinterland of magic in the private rituals and meditations by which you re-make the world in the inner vision or in private gatherings.

Deeper insight than this may lead you into understanding that what you call your self is also a construct, a cobbled-together organ which you grew to get you through the everyday world. The mundane self is not the most real part of you, and having that perspective enables you to know that the bad stuff in the world cannot pervert or destroy your essence.

This is wisdom.

Both magic and wisdom are filtering up from the private worlds of magic and art, and may be the best tools we have for mending the broken world.

The first time I burned a banknote it was a fiver, in 1971. I did it to prove a point, forcibly. The force of my proof came from the destruction of the money, money I could ill-afford to destroy. I succeeded in impressing my interlocutor, to the extent her jaw literally dropped and she repeatedly expressed disbelief at what I had done: blasphemed the Great Idol of capitalism—cash!

So I had given something up (food security for the next few days) to get what I felt at the time was something better (winning an argument about the viability of anarchy). That type of transaction is one definition of sacrifice. I had bought, with my £5, a memorable moment of ideological victory.

Not only had I performed a sacrifice, but also an act of blasphemy. By destroying that fiver I was showing that such an act is possible. What that amounted to was tearing off the blindfold that keeps us wage-enslaved, hypnotized into compliance with the ever-retreating carrot of security and the ever-credible stick of suffering, by refusing to take seriously that threat of suffering.

So even such an apparently simple act of money-burning has all sorts of ramifications. For a start, the power of the act can be seen as arising both from the external shock it caused and the change in my own internal state. The former is a result of having witnessed an act of blasphemy. The latter comes from at least two sources: my exhilaration at having performed a blasphemous act and my sense of having impoverished myself. Blasphemy and sacrifice, a fiver's worth at 1971 prices. Bargain!

From Snafu to Fubar: Five Spanners in the War-Machine

Another fruit of Festival 23 was a one-day event, 'Catch-23', at a club in town in 2018. We put together a magical working for it.

This working was what it said on the tin, to throw spanners in the global war-machine. One of the things about public rituals is that people may be there who have never done a group magical working, or any type of magical ritual, so more explanation is required as to the function of each part of the working. The overall working was described as 'a five-pronged sabotage of the effectiveness of the global war machine, in particular the danger that some idiot might actually try to use weapons of mass destruction.'

Then the title. SNAFU and FUBAR are of course military terms which gained some notoriety through Joseph Heller's anti-war novel *Catch-22*, and in the Discordian world through Robert Anton Wilson's introduction of the SNAFU Principle. This states that in rigid hierarchies, the further up the ranks you rise the less accurate your picture of the world becomes, because everyone is minding their status in the hierarchy and so only tells their superiors things they believe they want to hear. Hence the Situation is Normal, All Fucked Up. By the time you've progressed to FUBAR, nothing works at all—it's Fucked Up Beyond All Recognition. This is the fate we desired for the war machine, in the overall intention: 'It is our Will that weapons of mass destruction are never used.'

This working utilized music and dancing to raise the energy of five runestaves, each representing a separate but linked intention. We announced these and checked that everyone was on board:

ANSUZ 'The weapons don't work'
BERKANO 'When it comes to it, people won't push the button and launch WMDs'
WUNJO 'The laughter of the universe banishes the insanity of mass destruction'
RAIDHO 'In the eye of the real, how can this possibly happen?'
ISA 'The snow of ISA falls into military temples'

The space was prepared with a circle of masking tape and bowls of coloured powders—flour, paprika, blackseed and polenta. As we sang each rune, I made the shape in white powder inside the circle, gradually building up a bindrune. With each rune shape, I invited people to step into the circle and add colours and their own energies whilst each rune was being chanted.

The final stage involved dancing to George Rogers' music and chanting the bindrune sound WABRI until the runes were charged. We closed by banishing with laughter.

This spell became a servitor, and is on its way to becoming an egregore entity, which everyone is welcome to work with for the same purpose—to reduce the probability of WMDs ever being used. Its name is its bindrune sound, WABRI. It has a bindrune, which you can skry for an 'astral' form for:

If you do skry for its form, you will enrich it with your own input, and will be joining in with a cluster of people who have added their energy and awareness to it. If a lot more people do that, not just using the entity—in itself a good thing—but generating new perspectives of their own, that will increase its power and reach.

Egregore Entities for the World

One kind of magic you can't actually set going on your own is egregore work. Egregores are magical group minds, the esoteric aspect of the group mind, spirits with independent existence that were first assembled by a particular group.

I use the term 'egregore entity' because egregore to some people means deity, to others, simply group mind. It's not a servitor, it's something much more complex (see my earlier piece in Part 1, 'The Cyberzoo'). Such entities have degrees of freedom that seem to confer genuine sentience on them.

You won't find many records of egregore entities with this level of sentience in the magical literature, but one exception is the GOTOS, the egregore of the *Fraternitas Saturni,* a somewhat-Thelemic German magical order established in 1926. The order's founder, Eugen Grosche, aka Gregor A. Gregorius, was interned during the Nazi years and survived until 1964. The FS itself was revived after the war, with a somewhat different culture, and is still active.

As is their egregore, some say, which is perhaps not surprising considering that it was initially established and nourished with rituals involving sex magick and mescaline.

My first experience of collective-entity work was with the chaos group which became known as the Circle of Chaos, which ran in West Yorkshire from 1984 to '87. It was a science fiction theatre in which we each took on the roles of our future selves, much more powerful in magic, and from that standpoint spoke our egregore into being with poems and spontaneous invocations. It was a beautiful and moving ritual, the candlelit sanctuary, the golden glow of the statue, and a time-warp into the deep future. The entity was the most powerful spirit I had worked with at that stage. One example of its power (included in the list of my twelve most powerful workings in *Bright From The Well*) was an extraordinary legal victory. A friend and magical co-worker, wrongly accused, was advised by his lawyer to plead guilty. He rejected this advice and came to me to help him with some magical work, to take his case to Crown Court and get a full acquittal. We turned the egregore entity loose on the courtroom and instructed it to get my friend acquitted. I accompanied him into court, to observe and to add power to the entity, and shall never forget the happy, serene look on the Judge's face as he summed up. Basically, he told the jury to ignore the probably dubious attestations of the police and extend their sympathy to the plight of my friend. Against his lawyer's expectations, he was acquitted, and there in the courtroom I 'saw' the astral form of the egregore entity looming over the Bench.

Over a decade later, the earliest IOT egregore entity to be released to the public magical world was Kawa Pohr, our spirit for healing and regeneration. This entity took much longer to reach its full power, and then it became very impressive. It started humble: in 1993 I wrote a pathworking for my chaos magic group to produce a healing servitor. Two years later the entity was built up further at a bigger meeting, with more participants, and it got a sigil and a name—Kawa Pohr. It was made to be heuristic, learning from situations and thereby becoming more complex. The degrees of freedom it started exhibiting demonstrated that it has true chaos in its makeup, just like you and me.

There are some features we can identify of how egregore entities are made. First, you need a group; you can't make this sort of entity on your own. Second, you need to build chaos into it, to give it many degrees of freedom. There's a lot of difference between this sort of entity and a mere servitor. A servitor can be thought of as an 'astral machine', a simple set of instructions triggered by certain situations arising. It is not expected to make choices beyond a TOTE strategy, test-operate-test-exit. But an egregore entity will be expected to make certain judgment calls, so it needs to be imbued with enough chaos, enough raw mind-stuff, to be able to do so. This in turn means it will evolve and develop.

You end up with something which is likely to learn from situations and is able to shift its shape. It helped that we gave Kawa Pohr a quirky basic form—the white sphere emerging from the sea was suggested by the cult 1960s TV show *The Prisoner*. This amounts to giving it a kind of 'personality', an organ for dealing with the world.[46]

Another feature which seemed to help Kawa Pohr was skrying for its deep mythic history, letting it have a layer which suggests we didn't actually create it, but that it was a pre-existing powerful being. We didn't consciously make up any of the stuff about it living in a laser-green pyramid under the sea, that all came from visions, which overlapped rather impressively between different skryers who had not been in touch with each other. This was further evidence that it had already developed some degree of sentience.

Recordings of the Kawa Pohr pathworking can be found online.[47, 48]

We've worked with other big spirits in the IOT. One was co-created as a Chaos Spin Doctor, designed to rebalance certain features of the 'Operation Mindfuck' effect, the Discordian-originated breaking-down of consensus reality.

Another entity which was launched by the IOT in 2007 is still evolving. Some good results are being reported, but its mission is a tough one: to help with depression. The name VARRAWALLAL was extracted from a chaotic chant; this entity was born in chaos. There are three versions of the name because the entity has three aspects: mental process, physiological processes and pure magic / spirit. This is reflected in the form of its sigil.

You are invited to help develop this entity, by using it.

---

[46] Kawa Pohr history: https://iotbritishisles.com/2020/03/08/kawa-pohr-the-iots-healing-servitor/

[47] The Kawa Pohr pathworking with original sound: https://youtu.be/COOYbDdAhXs

[48] 'The Illuminates Of Thanateros - Evocation of Kawa Pohr' can be found on the IOT BIS YouTube channel, and provides a version with more elaborate sound.

VARRAWALLAL / FARRAWALLA / BARRAWALLAL an Anti-Depression Spirit

The original working had the intention of finding the name of the entity.

Its mission was: to overcome and alleviate depression.

This Statement of Intent was discussed carefully—the last thing we wanted to create was an entity that would *cause* depression in order to alleviate it, a pattern that I'm sure you're familiar with if you've ever met a poorly-designed servitor; the Sorcerer's Apprentice Syndrome.

We did glossolalia until their sounds converged on the Name of the entity, which was heard as VARRAWALLAL, FARRAWALLAL and BARRAWALLAL.

Gradually, the notion came to me that this entity was somehow triple in nature, with its three possible names. I wondered whether this threefold nature correlated to different facets of its work against depression. At that time, I tended to regard interventions into depression as consisting of two basic kinds—on the one hand, those techniques that help control of the internal monologue and thought processes, such as Cognitive Behavioural Therapy and some uses of NLP, and on the other, physiological interventions such as exercise, drugs and smart nutrients.

The third facet fell into place when I was depressed. A friend, a magician, talked me through a process in which I reached up to a higher state of consciousness. This was immediately effective: it gave me a different perspective on some of my issues. I realised that the third aspect of Varrawallal was that of a ladder to higher consciousness. This of course fits in with the use of psychedelics in depression therapy.

This third limb of the entity also relates to how we conceive of our daily life. If we go along with the usual bourgeois idea that life is about working for money, paying your bills (and debts), all iced over with the occasional but of fun and pleasure, then that is not a view of life which fulfils you as a human being. If you have no sense of agency and no higher perspective on your world, you will feel trapped. Also, mainstream society nudges us to follow news about world events about which we can probably have no effect on; this learned helplessness is one of the most insidious features of bourgeois society. We need to take back control of our newsfeed, unless we want to immerse ourselves in helplessness every day.

I made a sigil incorporating this threefold idea:

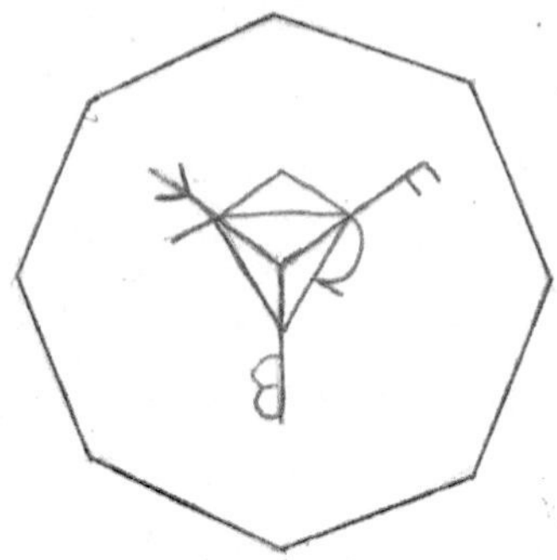

As for its visualized form, the starting point might be a pearl-grey polyhedron. But I get the distinct impression this being is a shapeshifter, adapting its appearance to what it works out to be the most useful form for each person it intervenes with.

The next time we used it a particularly astute participant pointed out that chanting its name fell naturally into the rhythm of the Doctor Who theme. This suggested another mode of action—the spirit can take you into your own past, to repair trauma memories and your attitude to them. (Like NLP Timeline therapy).

If you want to work with it, I suggest the following as starting points:

Find your own astral form for it; summon it and let your own mind give it shape.

Chant to the *Doctor Who* theme.

Follow up with regular work on higher consciousness, such as sitting meditation.[49]

[49] For a very brief rundown on the relationship between meditation and the rest of our lives, including mental health, see https://chaosmagick.com/meditation-for-magicians-a-brief-exploration/

Izawa History

IZAWA grew out of an entity created by a group I worked with in 2011. It started life as an 'Eight-Circuit Egregore', an expert in all the levels of consciousness defined by Timothy Leary and Robert Anton Wilson in the model of that name. Its initial brief was to assist and nurture our psychedelic gnoses. The eight best scripts for each level were chosen and inserted over five sessions. As we built the circuits in, we added glow-sticks to a sigil, then photographed it.

A few months later, the entity had a name—Izawa, and a mission—to nurture work with psychedelic sacraments. We started skrying to learn more of its nature and to find its form.

Later that year we developed its mission further—'To nurture, protect and expand the psychedelic gnosis in these islands'. This came out of our decision to do some magic to help the Santo Daime church with its legal problems in the UK, and mutated into doing something with Izawa to protect the psychedelic gnosis itself, and improve its legal position. From being a purely 'internal' advice servitor, Izawa becomes a being with a big job in the world. This was crystallized into a new mission: 'To introduce wisdom, truth and respect for evidence into the public drugs debate.' We also started gathering materials to make a statue.

From early in its development, we had always planned to introduce it to the wider magical world, via live events. In 2016 Izawa attended Festival 23, and in 2017 appeared in the Psychedelic Museum exhibition at the international psychedelics conference Breaking Convention.

Izawa was with Nikki Wyrd on the winter solstice of 2016 when she was injected with DMT at Imperial College London, and was present in 2019 when Julian Vayne took part in the psilocybin trial at King's College Hospital, London.[50]

Izawa has been present at other events too. Its travels around the world and into the imaginal realms continue.

---

[50] Thanks to Julian Vayne and Nikki Wyrd for information on the later history of Izawa. You can read more here; https://theblogofbaphomet.com/2019/08/17/tribes-get-high-power-practice-and-politics-in-the-psychedelic-renaissance/ and, https://theblogofbaphomet.com/2017/02/02/witch-on-dmt-for-science/

Arcanorium College and The Colours of Chaos

In 2006 Pete Carroll founded Arcanorium College, and recruited a stellar cast of teachers. I was delighted to be running courses alongside Lionel Snell, Ian Read, Lola Babalon, Julian Vayne and Jaq Hawkins.

It used a forum-like classroom structure, where students and lecturer met once a week for courses that typically lasted six or more weeks, sharing text and graphics in the lesson and discussing the results of their week's homework. The fact that the courses were all live and neither recorded not repeated meant that there was a creative pressure to write new courses, but eventually everyone was bound to run out of new material. That model meant that I originated a number of courses, some texts of which I incorporated into some of the courses I now offer on *Chaotopia School of Magic*. This is a different kind of teaching experience, more remote but with facilities to handle lifetime-access self-paced courses, which Arcanorium couldn't. This is one way the world of magical teaching has evolved.

Another development is the prevalence of Zoom meetings. Obviously, a physical-presence magical group meeting is never going to be equalled in intensity of either magic or conviviality by an online event, but it's better than no meeting at all, and it's very useful for the teaching of magical techniques. I've been offering courses via various online platforms, both live and lifetime-access, for a while now.

Arcanorium shrank to just Pete Carroll's magical qualification course in just a few years, but the initial experiment was valuable for those involved. It was a great environment for me to develop online teaching materials and skills, and in particular to extend my work on teaching energy magic. In Arcanorium, I ran three energy magic courses—'Introduction to Energy Magic', 'Breath, Gnosis and Energy' and 'The Dragon-Eagle Working'.[51] The latter I first wrote about in my Northern Mysteries book *Bright From The Well*. It is an exercise which uses symbolism from the Norse myths of the Tree of Yggdrasil and the beings that live upon it, as a model of the human energy system. The overall idea is similar in function to kundalini work.

Recently I discovered to my delight and awe how much energy magic can be accomplished without physical presence. In 2021 I presented a weekend webinar on energy magic for the *Occulture Berlin* online series.

Another course I ran at Arcanorium, 'Eight Retirements: Build Your Own Magical System' evolved directly from the following presentation. I did

[51] The material from those three courses is all in *Life Force*. The energy magic material has been run live with Viktor Wynd's online courses, and will be included in two forthcoming courses on Chaotopia School of Magic.

have a job deciding where to fit this piece in, because it could also have gone in Part 1, or because of the Northern Magic content, in part 2.

In 2008 at Colours of Chaos, a public IOT event at Conway Hall in London I presented a magical system which was very much my own, with a transparent structure that people could use to develop their own systems.

YOURSELVES—THE GRIMOIRE OF SELFHOOD, COLOURS OF CHAOS 2008

A COUPLE OF DEFINITIONS:

I use the term 'Grimoire' because this is about a personal system of spirit magick.

'Selfhood' is about how we view, and act upon, the community of apparent or illusory selves we each have.

BACKGROUND ON MULTIPLE SELVES:

When I was fairly new to magick I got intrigued by the idea that we have different identities in different contexts. The idea was there in the writings of Robert S. De Ropp, particularly his Gurdjieff-influenced *The Master Game*, in Richard Bandler's 'Parts Work', and in the writings of Pete Carroll. I wrote down facilely all the roles I play. I wasn't convinced that I'd generated anything useful with this list, and let it lie for a while.

Years later, after much more magick and meditation I got accustomed to the sense that I was watching all these selves from a standpoint that didn't feel like any of them. I appeared to observe from an empty place, a centre of the pantheon of selves.

I think those of you who recognize this experience in your own work will agree that it's impossible to continue in a naïve view of selfhood after such a radical, even though subtle, deconstruction of identity.

You can never say I AM again without asking who's speaking.

This eventually led to me rebuilding my entire self-complex over a series of magickal retirements, a concentrated series of daily magickal work. The result of this was my personal grimoire, my own system of spirit magick.

I'm going to describe the steps I took and the interpretations I laid on them. I'm not going to present a fait accompli, because that would be useless or worse than useless. If this story is of any use to anyone else its usefulness lies in the general ideas and stages of the process, not the specifics, which you'll have to create for yourself, meaningful only to you, if you choose to work in such a way.

Also, the wise organizers of this event have decided, wisely, to limit the amount of rambling by making sure nobody can go on for too long.

FORMING THE GRIMOIRE

Eschewing for the moment the invocation of the HGA—I may come back to this issue if there's time—I went for a metaphysically-minimalist approach. I started with no assumptions about my selves, but instead asked myself what qualities, what powers and faculties I wanted to exhibit in my life.

This is a bottom-up approach, rather than the top-down approach of HGA invocation.

I made a square card for each of these powers, painted with the sigil, bindrune or in some instances form of each power.

A few examples: a spirit to increase the skills I need for public speaking; a spirit for powerful, joyous work-rhythm, a spirit for healing and strength.

At the start, I had about fifteen spirits, and more came along as I worked.

EXERCISE: Maybe you'd like to think for a moment about the skills and abilities you might use in this stage.

As a further consideration, you might visualize them around you, spreading out from your centre in a kind of flat, circular plane.

I shall come on to the significance of the circular plane later (though it's probably obvious).

These spirits are analogous to helper spirits in shamanism, to some Goetic spirits in renaissance magick. I sometimes think of them as the wights called Dwarves in the Northern magickal tradition.

Also, these spirits contain mundane considerations, so from a psychological model they can be thought of as related to Strategies in NLP, sets of sequential instructions to the subconscious mind. However, NLP is not magick, and these spirits also contain magickal instructions. If I need assistance from outside my own skin or to influence the external world magickally, these spirits can provide it—that is implicit in all of them, however mundane their apparent sphere of influence.

This circle of Dwarves now constitutes a basic, mundane-magick level of my personal Grimoire. The square cards represent the most basic functional level of spirits, one's personal skills or powers. They are not selves.

One of the magically-interesting features of such spirits is that you can share them—we all know that spirits require attention from humans to prosper and remain effective, and if more people are paying attention to them it empowers them more. I share a number of my spirits with my chaos magick group.

The next stage was to create or recognize a spirit that harmonizes all the complex needs and energies of the dwarf-squares. At first, I had only that idea—to create something to harmonise it all. But, in considering the relation an entity would have to be in to these spirits to do that job, it's obvious that it would have to be a more complex spirit with more degrees of freedom, more power, more flexibility. In fact, it was more or less by definition my Magickal Self. This I represented with an octagonal card.

This level, this octagon, is not only more complex—'higher,' if you like—than the dwarf-squares, but higher too than the Selves. How come? Because it contains within itself the core of the self-making faculty, the faculty of identifying with some spirit and thereby making it YourSelf for as long as that identification persists.

So where do the Selves fit in this circular model?

In complexity, they lie between the square and the octagon, and I represented them by hexagons.

They are at the root of the powers of each of the Dwarf-squares; to explain this, let me take on example. I came to realise that my dwarf-spirit for joyous work rhythm is exactly what I wanted to identify with in work-mode. I therefore made it the core of my Orange, Mercurial self, concerned with work and intellect.

The circular model now extends to incorporate the selves.

EXERCISE: You might like to visualize your powers radiating out from points of identity, which are each of your selves, still on a flat plane. Maybe a public self, a work self, a sex self, a conflict self and so on.

Of course, each self has its demonic facets—there's a Neptunian self for mysticism and a Neptunian demon of inappropriate drug use, an Orange self of work and intellect and an Orange demon of overwork and mental obsession, and so on.

The Magickal self, the Octagon, does not fit on this plane. With the Octagon of the magickal self, our spirit model has now moved out from the flat, circular plane of mundane magicks and acquired a vertical dimension. To represent some of what is happening here I'll introduce a traditional model I've found immensely useful: the tree Yggdrasil in the Norse mythos.

THE CREATURES OF YGGDRASIL

The dragon is the impersonal life-force, the instincts, the churning powers of life and death, the serpent-force at the root of the spine; it is pre-personal, and immortal. It is fed by ecstasy and danger—it doesn't care if your particular body lives or dies, as long as the experience is intense.

The eagle is the magickal self—the archetypal magician-god Odin has, as one of his poetic names, 'Eagle-headed'.

The squirrel is the babbling internal monologue, passing to the eagle the dragon's message of mortality, that our death is scripted in our flesh.

The harts[52] are the daily stresses and attritions that eat away at the trunk of our mundane world.

[52] A hart is a mature red deer stag.

The hawk is the watchfulness of the gods, the observing faculty (sometimes called the observer self) that sits above the tumult of the Tree and its beings. It is glyphed by Austin Spare as a vulture, the Kia or atmospheric I, hovering over the feast of life and death.

I prefer to be cautious about using the term 'observing self' because this faculty is so unlike the other, mundane selves. The mundane selves are illusions of selfhood suited to objectified commerce with the mundane world. They are contracted selves, with outlines. They can be seen as objects, can be studied by mundane psychology, because they are not fully conscious—though they'd have you think they are. They engage in limited cycles of predictable behaviour. They run us most of the time, when we are on automatic, when we are asleep in the Gurdjieffian sense.

They are trapped in cycles of self-reference. They claim the energies of your body and spew out the particular patterns of emotional and mental states we associate with each of those selves. They are illusory. In the language of chaos magic, they are Choronzon, misidentification, the demons in the abyss of hallucination, and it is important to bear this in mind when working with them.

Ramsey Dukes's excellent *Little Book of Demons* deals with how to negotiate with them. In the process of negotiating with them, you will notice that the point-of-attention that is doing the communicating with them is the point around which you are building your magical self. The perspective from which you communicate with the demon-selves is the core of the magickal self.

The demon-selves are, if you like, the walls around specific trances. The observing faculty is the opposite of trance, is the core of awakened consciousness. From this perspective, you see all your selves, you are viewing your inner ecosystem from the point of view of the Eye of the Hawk. The Hawk's name is Vedhrfolnir, which can be translated as 'storm-bleached'—it has no qualities, is a bright point of attention. When you dive down into identification with one or other of them you are in trance again, walled in by the concerns of that self.

Incidentally, the dangers of the path of invoking the HGA arise from misidentifying it as a self in the same sense as the mundane selves, just 'Higher' in some way. The worst example of this sort of Choronzonic nonsense I can think of was the advice by one of those old-school magicians, I think William Gray, which is to project what you see as your 'best' qualities onto the Higher Self. This strikes me as pure *mauvais foi*, pure delusion. The genuine end of the HGA current must rely on the reshuffling of identity in the throes of some transpersonal ecstasy. All you'll be invoking with the Gray formula is your ego in its Sunday best, with Choronzon right up your fundament.

So we now have a vertical complement to our horizontal plane. We privilege the observing faculty that is cultivated through magick and meditation, the Eye of the Hawk whose name is Storm-Bleached.

EXERCISE: Maybe you'd like to visualize this expanded configuration: a vertical axis pierces the horizontal plane of the selves and the dwarves, and at the top of it is your observing faculty. At the root of the vertical is the dragon, the impersonal life-force. Between them, the deer nibble and the squirrel runs...

Now I'm going to look at a couple more speculative models of the spirits of selfhood.

What functions do we have so far in our Grimoire?

- we have the mundane selves and their powers on a horizontal plane
- we have the higher, untranced consciousness of the Hawk

To complete our scale of magickal functions I think we need one more kind of ability: what is often called soul-retrieval.

Consider all the people you've loved, and/ or been in love with. You give each of them part of your attention, part of your being. Sometimes, you neglect to recover that part of yourself when your lives separate.

It might be useful to think of these as parallel lives, as separate tracks of your love-life.

Consider all the skills you've used in the careers you've followed. I could have been a perfume chemist, a teacher, a businessman, a healer.

It might be useful to think of these as separate, parallel tracks of your work-life.

Think of the times when, as a magician, you've tried to change your behaviour in some quite drastic fashion—maybe stopping smoking or dealing with some other addictive phenomenon.

The vow you take is one track; if you break it, you resume the track you left behind and split your life once more.

All of these splits can be thought of as soul-loss.

Recovering those lost souls starts with becoming aware of the parallel tracks they exist on.

EXERCISE: Maybe you'd like to give some thought to the times you were split, when your life forked into two timelines. Honour these timelines by visualizing them as parallel, vertical threads running through the horizontal plane of your selves.

Just so that I don't end up on a neat note of apparent finality—because that would be unrealistic in this wild world—I'll end with a few questions and random thoughts.

First, some spirits just turn up unbidden, and sometimes they're very useful.

For instance, I have a spirit I call the Inner DJ. This plays songs, usually ones I like, and eventually the persistence of the song is such that I listen to which lyrics are being accentuated. Then I check if that theme is reflected in any of my current obsessions and treat them as a guide to clarifying that issue.

Also, bearing in mind that the Dwarf or Servitor spirits can be shared with other magicians, why not the Selves? Oh no, you might think—those are ME! But really, aren't they ultimately empty, ultimately generic?

Also, consider the uses of the Black Self, the Death Self—this can become, *à la* Castaneda, your greatest advisor. Once your survival is relativised by a full-on encounter with the Black, it makes it much easier to become aware of your self in every detail of what you do in life. Your capacity to observe, to transcend, is vastly enhanced.

Finally, it might be worth considering that the most creative things you ever do come not from any self you can name, but from somewhere else, on the empty edge of your consciousness, some place where everything is always being improvised.

Healing Magics and Body Alchemy

Some of my publicly available magical healing work is bundled up into a course on the Chaotopia School of Magic. One of the exercises on that course is a bit of aura magic.

In 1980, when I was first learning magic, a friend talked me through the Middle Pillar exercise first popularized by Israel Regardie. That exercise consists of building an image of your aura in the form of the Middle Pillar on the Qabalistic Tree of Life. You can then circulate energy, drawing on the powers of each sephirah to strengthen and cleanse your aura. It was just the right time for me to learn this exercise, and it had a pleasantly dramatic effect—I could feel the different levels of my being slotting neatly together. Later that year at the Mushroom Fair in mid-Wales I watched the same friend talk a distressed, psychedelically shaken young woman who'd wandered into our encampment through a simplified version of it, with immediate beneficial effect. She sort of came into focus, smiled, said, 'Oh, thank you', and walked away.

The Middle Pillar became part of my daily practice, and was also my go-to resource for when I was processing a difficult encounter or generally feeling ragged. This type of exercise also sharpens your sensitivity not only to the condition of your own aura but to the energetic transactions happening around you.

The following is the introduction to a non-denominational energy-centres working, much simpler than the exercises in the 'Dragon-Eagle Working', published in *Bright From the Well*. It's available on YouTube.[53]

---

[53] Energy-centres audio pathworking The Column of Lights is at https://youtu.be/efGDnejuRcw

AURA WORK

First of all, it's worth saying that when people talk about the aura, they mean a number of different things; and this doesn't matter for what we will be doing. You don't need to know much about what your aura is or what it might be in order to influence it, and that's what the Column Of Lights video is about. In any event, knowing only a little puts us in the same boat as everyone else who talks about the aura—no-one knows everything about it, because it's a mystery.

But if you follow certain procedures, it doesn't matter what you think, because something real will happen!

Some levels of the aura produce effects that you can measure with physical equipment—electromagnetic fields and so forth—but these are secondary. The most interesting levels of the aura can't be measured with machines, but that is where the real power is. These powerful parts of the aura seem to consist purely of imagination, but if we work with them, these imaginal structures have real effects on your health and strength and many other parts of your life.

That is because your aura comprises a complex symbol, sculpted in living energy, of the state you are in—including your health, your physical vitality, the integrity of your personal defences and the way you relate to others.

That's why some healers talk about reading auras. When someone reads an aura, that person is picking up something about you and the way their deep mind informs them of that is by generating a colour picture of your aura where the details show them what the issues are. That is a receptive use of a personal model of the aura.

Conversely, we can make active use of an aura model. Using that picture, you can have real effects on these parts of your life. You can enhance your physical and mental health.

The picture I'm supplying you for this work is twofold: One level of it is the image of five energy centres arranged from the base of the spine to the crown of the head. These represent levels of consciousness, like the chakras, to which they're related. The column that joins them is the superhighway of cosmic energy as it is processed through you. Each of these centres is rich in symbolism, but a basic outline of what they mean is as follows:

The base centre is Earth, your physical being. The crown centre is Spirit, your infinite and eternal nature. The centre one-place-up from the base is energy, sex and emotion. The centre one-down from the top is conscious mind and speech. The middle centre is both your heart and your world—everything in your experience, right now, integrating all the other levels into the present moment.

The other level of your aura we are working with is the field that surrounds you. This symbolizes and carries the energies of your health, both mental and physical, and your social world, how you interact with others. If your boundaries are weak, it will be represented somewhere on your aura-field. If you are mentally troubled, the field may be disturbed, turbulent. If you are sick, there may be gaps or weak, discoloured areas in the field. The Energy Fountain takes the cosmic energy that is flowing through you all the time, concentrates it and spreads it over your external field to repair, strengthen and balance it.

A Pair of Spirits

As I wrote above, some kinds of servitors are better for being shared, even those that have not been designed to becoming egregore entities. Here are two you might find useful.

HIRXIL-NU: A SERVITOR FOR EMOTIONAL-CREATIVE ALCHEMY

You know when you've got an exciting project to get to work on, but you are stuck in some other set of feelings? Try this working. It involves some qigong movements, see for instance.[54]

The instruction for the servitor is: to transmute, on instruction, any emotion into the enthusiasm and passion needed for creating.

Recall any great feelings of creative work.

Chant HIRXIL-NU a few times, draw the sigil out, trace its outlines, internalize it.

Invite the servitor in: 'Watch, listen and learn your tasks, new servitor HIRXIL-NU'

Do *baduan-jin* exercise for Lungs, 3 x, declaring 'I transmute depression and negativity'

Do *baduan-jin* exercise for Liver, 3 x, declaring 'I transmute anger and hate'

Do *baduan-jin* exercise for Spleen-pancreas, 3 x, declaring 'I transmute worry and anxiety'

Do *baduan-jin* exercise for Kidney, 3 x, declaring 'I transmute fear'

You may continue with a litany of personal statements such as: 'When I feel pissed off, I'd rather be creating!' 'When I feel [*choose emotion*] I'd rather be creating!'

Declare: 'Any emotions I wish, I transmute by calling your name, visualizing your sigil or using your mantra—HUH-HUH! into the passion of creating! HIRXIL-NU, this is your task! Do it whenever I summon you!

[54] I put movements from Baduanjin together with Qigong Healing Movements, as learned from Eric Yudelove's 2002 book *100 Days to Better Health, Good Sex and Long Life: Guide to Taoist Yoga* which, despite its title, is actually very good.

SORU: A SERVITOR FOR CULTIVATING A HEALTHY LIFESTYLE

SORU is built around a bindrune of Younger Runes Ur, Reidh and Sol, and is another servitor designed to act on yourself, to cultivate a taste for exercise, healthy diet and other aspects of a healthy lifestyle. It has been in use for years, and needs only to be called, visualized and personally instructed.

Afterwords: Now and Then

In this book I've touched on a few varieties of practical magic. But it's important to keep in mind that magic is not just about instrumental capacity. It's not simply for making things happen, as thrilling and awe-inspiring as that is, and as significant as the results of sorcery are in showing us how we relate to the universe at large.

My original interest in magic, fanned to life by the flames of teenage acid trips, started with an interest in higher consciousness, the idea that life could actually be radically better at every level of experience, and that this could come about by inner work. Which is something I got the basic idea of at age 18, but took me a few decades to start making it real. In the meantime, in my mid-20s, I was wooed by magic's promise of power, of enhanced effectiveness, of the expansion of my life in various directions. At that stage, magic was mostly a tool.

After a few years, I outgrew that narrow perspective. But instrumentalism is not entirely a dead end: that approach to the world is deeply embedded in Western myth—Faust and, in a certain sense, Prometheus. That magical pragmatism, brought back into the history of magic by the chaos current, was a massive refreshment to the tired psychologizing of the predominant magical scene of the 1950s.

But eventually most magicians get tired of just doing spells, and wondering how to apply more sheer power to their desire. This disenchantment with enchantment, this *spell-fatigue*, leads to questioning what one's magic is for, where it's going.

With some of us, that question turns into a tendency to see magic as another kind of thing. Much of Pete Carroll's work gives the impression he wants to turn magic into a branch of physics. I'm not entirely immune to that allure—I practised science for some years, and still have a love for its best features, and magic has some very interesting interfaces with its younger sister. But it ain't the same beast; physics cannot fully embrace the wildness of lived experience. What's more, making magic scientifically respectable and therefore part of the mainstream discourse would carry its own risks, not the least of which would be that it would provide the police with another excuse to persecute people. Wizards would be subject to their doors getting kicked in.

Alan Moore claims that magic is always art; but art is a pursuit which requires an audience other than yourself, or it's surely not art, but magic.

Some magicians emphasise the aspects of magic which border on religion. Alan Chapman takes very seriously Aleister Crowley's dictum, which goes something like 'All magic is black magic unless it is directly concerned with the Holy Guardian Angel' and insists that the *real* magick is faith, an intricate faith that involves deciphering the obscure communications of divine intelligences.

Other writers seem to think that magic needs to be improved by academic discourses. To my mind that sucks all the juice out of it, turns it into grist for Scientism's Dark Satanic Mill. Yet others see magic primarily through the lens of changing the world, a perspective which is vitally important, but which can never be the whole story.

Magic is fascinating because it is protean, a shapeshifting weird thing at the edges of our perception and ideation, slippery, with ineffable bits. That's how come people can write all the above kinds of things about it, and lay claim to some kind of truth.

For much of my magical career I've swung between practical magic and the magic of higher consciousness, between a fascination with, and a contemptuous rejection of mysticism. I've generally rejected religion as a shell of political authority built around a living but neglected core of genuine spiritual insight. Much of mystical discourse is contaminated with religious ideology, of which the most significant element may be the rejection of embodied experience. Mainstream culture still carries an immense freight of anti-flesh ideology which reaches us from some of Plato's ideas, which were taken up by Augustine as the Christian church abandoned its ecstatic and joyous early stage and launched into centuries of relentless oppression and persecution.

Over the years I came to think there must be *something* in the idea of spiritual awakening or enlightenment, but that it seemed like some exotic state that could only be reached by devoting the entirety of your life (and other lives too if you believe in them). That negative view was reinforced by going on a vipassana retreat in 2005; as well as the ten days of silence and the many hours per day of sitting, we had to watch DVDs of Mr Goenka lecturing us about vipassana. In these lectures, he said we needed to practice for a minimum of two hours a day for many lifetimes to have a chance at enlightenment. This posits the idea of enlightenment and then locates it as more or less unattainable. I have an immense amount of respect for Goenka—he introduced meditation into the Indian prison system and probably saved many lives thereby. Maybe his recommendations are modelled on the life of a prison inmate.

From around 2011 my magical life swung back towards the mystical pole. Sometimes it just takes one phrase to crystallize a whole roomful of half-formed thoughts. It was the phrase 'the structure of experience' in Aaron

Daniels' book *Imaginal Reality,*[55] that brought the language of mysticism into focus for me in a new way. The structure of experience is exactly what we are absorbed in when we are in the dhyana or absorption stage of meditation, absorbed in the intimate experience of your awareness moving from one moment to the next.

Around that time I started learning meditation from Alan Chapman, whom I met through the chaos magic scene.[56] I took a vow to meditate daily, indefinitely. After six months I really started to get a taste for it, and after five years I started having a series of very interesting shifts in my worldview.

Daily meditation will eventually change you, especially if you are a seeker and enter into it expecting deep change. It may prove far from metaphysically neutral: you may have experiences which challenge your current model of the universe you're living in. This happens because you're soaking daily in the layer of consciousness immediately underneath the babble of your narrative self. Eventually this will move your mental centre of gravity to this level. You can get ambushed by deep transformation, as a result of the self-undoing features of mindfulness and related styles of meditation.

This is not actually a bad thing. It is after all what meditation is for in mystical contexts. But it can be emotionally challenging—all the old imprints you've got, all the thinking patterns that stop you making that shift of perspective will eventually arise and need to be dealt with.

It also means that the metaphysical picture of the universe, of reality, which you've unconsciously lived by will be challenged. Integrating that challenge into a new model of your experience, a new metaphysical framework, a new organic truth you can live from, will (hopefully) disrupt your understanding of categories such as body, mind, and spirit. Finding again and again truths we can live from is our best defence against the madness of the world.

For instance, the problem of death; one cultural response to that fear is the loathing of embodied experience. This horrific word virus thrived in the body of the Christian churches, and now reappears in a new guise: the idea that we will be able to cheat death by uploading ourselves into computers. The absurdity and horror of this idea are easily revealed with a few questions: *Whose computer? Who designs the afterlife? Who is paying?* From this perspective, the uploading heaven is the ultimate scam of the *rentier* phase of capitalism.

---

[55] Daniels A & L. (2011). *Imaginal Reality: Journey to the Voids*, Aeon Books.

[56] For my review of his 2019 book *Magia*, and some of my experiences, see https://chaotopia-dave.blogspot.com/2021/06/magia-teachings-of-alan-chapman.html

The proper response to this sort of nonsense is to turn away and live in the flesh. Make your peace with the idea of your own death, rather than chase the money in order to enter some ersatz heaven with a 'Meta' or 'X' brand stamped on every virtual tree.

The flesh is limiting, when viewed through the eyes of time; it's demanding, when viewed through the eyes of addiction; it's infinite, when seen from the heights. You don't often come across this position, such a fusion of what some would code as Left and Right-hand Paths. The artist who comes first to mind is William Blake, when he writes: 'Man has no Body distinct from his soul; for that called Body is a portion of a Soul discerned by the five senses, the chief inlets of Soul in this age.'

I've been practising magic as a conscious activity for over 40 years. I've read shedloads of books. I've travelled to various countries for meetings. I've suffered the grief of facilitating magical groups, as well as the immense joy. What have I got to show for it? My whole life, basically. My life, which is still going on, thankfully, in this body. Judging by what I've done, the main purpose of my life so far seems to have been to get people together to do weird things, things that have not yet been named.

That approach to life has been practical. As for the question of truth, I prefer to live with a degree of uncertainty, because I don't want a final, fixed answer. Chaos magic approaches its death via decadence when people try to make systems out of it, systems like the Golden Dawn's. There are always loose ends. This collection is not representative of where my magic is at the moment; looking back, I'm pleased to find myself disagreeing with many things I said 20–40 years ago. Had that not happened, I'd be concerned that I'd got stuck. A friend (who doesn't claim authorship) has said more than once that you have to keep moving, or the next tide washes away your footprints in the sand. I happen to know he wasn't talking about fame, but about your own growth, as well as the impact you make on the world.